the language of fashion design

S

746.92
VoL

First published in the United States of America in 2014 by
Rockport Publishers, a member of
Quayside Publishing Group
100 Cummings Center
Suite 406-L
Beverly, Massachusetts 01915-6101
Telephone: (978) 282-9590
Fax: (978) 283-2742
www.rockpub.com
Visit RockPaperInk.com to share your opinions, creations, and passion for design.

Library of Congress Cataloging-in-Publication Data available

10 9 8 7 6 5 4 3 2 1

ISBN: 978-1-59253-821-8

Digital edition published in 2014
eISBN: 978-1-61058-898-0

Design: Poulin + Morris Inc.
All photography www.shutterstock.com, unless otherwise noted.
Cover image: Getty Images/www.gettyimages.com

Printed in China

Laura Volpintesta

the language of fashion design

26 Principles
Every Fashion Designer
Should Know

Rockport Publishers
100 Cummings Center, Suite 406L
Beverly, MA 01915

rockpub.com • rockpaperink.com

S

contents

lan·guage \ˈlaŋ-gwij,\ *n*

1 a: the words, their pronunciation, and the methods of combining them used and understood by a community

2 b: form or manner of verbal expression; *specif*: style

The Language of Fashion Design takes its form in twenty-six chapters or principles, imitating the standard alphabet. Like the alphabet, this book aims to arm the reader with the building blocks to create new combinations from these twenty-six elements. While several of these elements are occurring simultaneously in any particular design featured herein, like characters in a word, use each chapter principle as a lens through which to view that particular principle while analyzing and observing it in action, for a firsthand experience.

    The captions beneath each image function as pointers, guiding the viewer to see how the element works within it. As a student, designer, and a teacher, what has always amazed me in the visual arts is the rite of passage that occurs every time I am giving or given "new eyes." Having been on both sides of this experience, I am delighted by the power that comes when a new vision is bestowed, and the student is able to see things (undercurrents, elements, energies) that they simply were not aware of before. Having learned three languages and having taught English as a second language as well, I can attest that the experience is no different in the visual arts, a language like any other.

Language has always been a marvelous key that unlocks doors, worlds, and minds. The mind connects with others that speak a language in a way that comes from sharing culture and experience through knowledge and memories. This book communicates the verbal, visual, analytical language of fashion by using fabric, construction, text, and imagery to define its elements.

Verbal and written language certainly have their limits: Words have perhaps always been an overly simple, yet culturally revered, way to express facts, feelings, and ideas. In selecting twenty-six elements here, it was a challenge to edit and select the dominant design principles. I chose the words that come up constantly in my teaching and design practice. But when those simple words are exemplified, what they speak about is unattainable in definitions; there is so much more in this book than words. Each design tells a story and carries a soul, as expressed through fashion design's aesthetics, technical aspects, emotions, values, and ideas communicated in a concept, presentation, or way of doing business. Words communicate, and behind the words there is a voice, and a receptor. As in all visual arts, the final ingredient to completing the experience is the viewer, with their own analysis, interpretation, and emotional response to the item's communication.

While researching thousands and thousands of images for this book, along with hundreds of biographies, it became obvious that there could not be a totally objective book about fashion. My personal experience as a human, student, and teacher, along with my particular generation and formative years in relation in time to fashion history, were inextricable from the task. No matter how hard I tried, I had to choose my values to have an angle. What came to the fore were the following:

1.   To reflect the range of styles that my students have brought to me over the past fifteen years, and thus represent a range of voices to appeal to each of the major categories of interest, from soft, elegant formalwear to hard-edged streetwear, from frilly to geometric and everything in between. Each look or line reminded me of the enthusiastic students I've had the honor of working with. Hopefully, there is something in here for all design perspectives.

2.   To dig into the current era and really pull out what is new, exciting, and relevant with my well-trained eye. I realized that the designers I grew up adoring have already been featured in all of the books and magazines I grew up studying so

intensely. This book should be relevant now and for years to come, not steeped in the past. As Isabel Toledo says: "Fashion is time." This book should be about now.

3. To feature a wide range of designers and countries, to stay away from megatrends and represent a wider range of voices, ages, and references. I wanted to represent well-known designers but balance that with fantastic, lesser-known voices who are doing great work globally and inspire the reader to learn more about them. It was fascinating to learn about so many new designers and markets in fashion weeks happening all over the globe, every day, and follow their stories. There is so much more out there than we can even imagine!

4. To focus on womenswear and healthy, life-affirming design images and businesses in a challenging era. I selected models to represent the full global range of nationalities that make up the fashion world, its design and production, representative of my students and our planet, while featuring designers who represent a healthy body image on their runways.

5. To include nondigital illustrations to maintain the interest and art of hand-drawn garment sketches alive, inspiring readers to create their own art.

6. To make sure that the biographies discuss philosophies, processes, business models, sustainability, and philanthropy, as current as possible to keep them relevant to designers working today and going forward; representing practical realities, as well as visionary and inspirational voices. Good womenswear design speaks to and improves women's lifestyles.

What was really a delightful surprise in my research was to find that so many designers go straight to the word *language*, especially when advising new designers to "develop their own language" based on trial and error in the design process. This can happen on the mannequin with scissors and pins, on paper with pencil, in the selection of fabrics, in marketing, business model, production methods, or how available resources are used to tell a story. This book can't do that part for you. But it is chock-full of images and stories of those who have, and through following their visual and written stories, I hope it will encourage you to take this vocabulary forward to refine your own unique language of fashion.

col·or \ kuhl-er \ *n*

1: the quality of an object or substance with respect to light reflected by the object, usually determined visually by measurement of hue, saturation, and brightness of the reflected light.

1

Color, despite a dry dictionary description, is very difficult to separate from emotion. We can discuss its theory and properties, but in the end what it conveys to us is emotional not technical. From the bleakest wash of gray sky to a flag emblazoned

with contrasting brights, from colors found in nature to the latest synthetic capabilities of color production, its fashionable value is found primarily in our emotional response to it. Designer Isabel Toledo sums it up well when she says she is not visual and that her use of color is entirely emotional.

The appearance of a color is always, in fact, affected by the colors it is viewed with. We experience colors relatively. For example, colors directly opposite one another on the wheel are called complementary colors. They naturally intensify each other. Red appears more red near green, orange appears more (continued on page 16)

Stained glass adornments pull the colors of the spectrum out of their source: pure, white light. Sculptural pieces with metal embellishments are the Georgia-born designer's trademark.

DAVID KOMA,
London, UK

Here, in some of de la Prada's simpler shapes, joyous color is the focus, played up to the maximum using palettes based on color theory. Orange and blue are complementary; blue, green, and yellow are analogous.

Agatha Ruiz de la Prada

MADRID

An utter declaration of intentions, the forms interact with their inhabitants, they generate new spaces between the body and the garment, between the individual and the environment, awakening sensations and concerns among observers and the observed; provoking, amazing and even fascinating but utterly incapable of leaving one indifferent. Garments for thinking and feeling." —Agatha Ruiz de la Prada on her designs

De la Prada's sense of emotional color and style is original, invigorating, and full of life season after season, as is her creativity in exploring shapes and themes in unconventional, whimsical ways that remind us how constrained the fashion design industry has become in comparison. She does not follow trends yet is always relevant and innovative, a touchstone for excellence in design.

With an immediately recognizable style, she has collaborated with countless iconic brands and associations in her totally unique voice on everything from bicycles to bedding, the holiday street lighting for the city of Madrid, building façades, murals, interiors, and public art for major cities. She designed a chemical-free dress for Greenpeace, as well as a dress for Minnie Mouse's eightieth birthday celebration.

In addition to de la Prada's sense of structure and timeless, trend-resistant color, she has a unique way of using and reinterpreting trademark motifs of hearts, stars, moons, candy, dinosaurs, umbrellas, and flowers (among others) in a graphic, playful, feminine riot. Her runways are also boldly self-designed.

She aims to provoke and amaze, describing her designs as "contemporary, abstract, pop, surreal, happy, and above all, positive." Her mission is "optimism through art and design." She began as part of the moda Madrileña scene, an expressive, hedonistic cultural movement in 1980s Spain marking the lifting of taboos after the death of the Franco regime. Pedro Almodóvar was also part of this scene.

While sometimes labeled "childlike" in her aesthetic, this should never be confused with simplicity without sophistication. Her work is childlike only in its undiluted enthusiasm and directness. The "retrospective" link on her website relentlessly offers up mind-boggling architectural and dressmaking techniques combined with expert, emotional journeys in color, totally rethought garment constructions and deconstructions that truly revive one's interest in garment design. Her designs seem to be in a public service of aesthetics, delight, and curiosity.

She uses pop and industrial fabrics, fine natural fibers, and nontraditional materials like cardboard, straw, vinyl, and wire. Many kinds of silk are used, raw, triple organza, gazar, satin, and raw silk coated with transparent sequins, to name a few.

Observing de la Prada's work, one sees a great sense of spirit and a fresh, sincere approach to fashion.

Color basics: the color wheel. Technically, all colors come from white. The visual effect of spinning the color wheel, amazingly, is white. The center triangle contains the three primary hues of red, yellow, and blue. (These colors are the basis for mixing all other colors.) Each primary, when combined with its neighbor, will produce the secondary round of hues: orange, violet, and green. The outer ring includes the tertiary colors ("the colors between the colors": red-orange, yellow-orange, yellow-green, and blue-green).

orange near blue, and so on. With this knowledge, a designer can manipulate our perceptions of colors, playing their intensity up or down. A split complementary color theme takes a color and works it with the two colors adjacent to its complement. Interestingly, a color pigment mixed with its complement will lose its brightness, eventually resulting in a dull, neutral, muddy color.

Colors that appear to move toward the viewer or relate to fire and warmth (red, orange, yellow) are referred to as warm colors, and colors that recede in the field of view or relate to cold (blue, green, violet) are called cool. Likewise, white expands and

Saturated, undiluted hues of pure color in contrasting geometric and flowing, abstract patterns against a black ground juxtapose stable and flowing motifs in a striking color story, straight off the wheel, on a reflective base fabric.

HERNAN ZAJAR,
Bogotá, Colombia

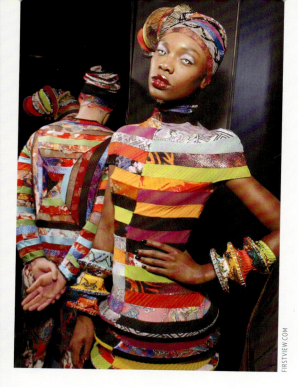

FIRSTVIEW.COM

Emotive yet careful piecing of solid and patterned fabrics in pure hues, pastels, and black highlights craftsmanship, the art of printed fabric, and the unique story that a selection of colors/prints can tell when combined, while the generous helping of pieces and fabrics rebels against mass production's often bland practicality.

LINO VILLAVENTURA,
Fortaleza/São Paulo, Brazil

comes forward visually while black recedes and shrinks. Colors mixed with white or black can have similar effects. (This is a feeling, not a fact, when looking at a flat surface, of course. In this way, color can create illusions of form.) A designer can use these effects to enhance the garment's shape and even to create illusions that mask or emphasize parts of the body or look.

A color mixed with any degree of white results in tints or pastels. Colors mixed with gray are called *tones*. Any color mixed with any quantity of black is called a *shade*.

When two colors mix to create a third color, placing this third color between them

creates an illusion of transparency and over-lapping color layers. When fabrics are woven with the warp yarns in one color and the weft yarns in another, or cross-dyed, the resulting fabric is iridescent as the colors blend and separate visually when the fabric moves.

Emotionally, colors can have a hard edge or a soft appeal. They can say "talk to me" or "I'm hiding." They also often have time periods and cultures attached to them, as every era and place has its own inherent universe of color. Technology, production methods, and materials always have an impact on fashion color. Planned obsoletion in the industrial era makes design colors

A street fashion blogger captures this ensemble highlighting the effect that complementary colors have on each other, as red and green vibrate in contrast to one another.

AMRIT JAIN,
Delhi, India

COURTESY OF AMRIT JAIN

Croquis book, in gouache and pencil, explores a color-blocked theme that uses transparency, both actual (layering sheer fabric color over color) and illusory (blocking pairs of opaque colors and using a third color to create the illusion of transparency).

PAULINA VIRGEN,
Calexico, CA, USA

identifiable by their time, and then changes the color trends so that past colors appear outdated and disposable, driving consumers back to the store.

   With this in mind, avoiding trends is the most sustainable method of color use, as is using sustainable methods to print and dye fabrics. Fashion colors rely on the properties of natural and synthetic fibers, skins, proteins, and filaments, as well as natural and chemical dye technologies, which also impact water supply and air quality through their production and life cycle of maintenance and disposal. In this way, color can address ethical concerns in sustainable fashion.

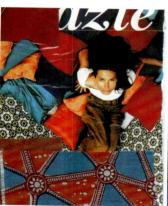

Each look in this group is completely monochromatic silk with a play of transparency against opacity. Most of the colors here are subdued by mixing with shades of gray. Notice the range of values in the collection.

NATALIA DOLENKO,
Kiev, Ukraine/London, UK

Inspiration boards featuring fabric swatches and magazine tears show balanced interplay of warm and cool tones, in solid and patterned surfaces.

LAURA VOLPINTESTA,
New York, NY, USA

shape \ sheyp \ *n*
1: the quality of a distinct object or body in having an external surface or outline of specific form or figure. **2:** this quality as found in some individual object or body form. Something seen in outline, as in silhouette.

2

Fashion is a form of sculpture. Amazingly, it works with a medium weight (fabric) that is basically two-dimensional, to create three-dimensional silhouettes and shapes, whether on the garment's surface, in the shaping of its components, and/or

in its overall appearance. In the atelier, fabric is either cut flat by instinct, with flat patterns, or draped on a dressform or model to create the patterns for reproduction—there is no absolute method, and there are many approaches. Individual pattern pieces that come out of the creation process are a set of two-dimensional shapes that, joined together, build the three-dimensional one.

The basic fitted pattern shapes are called slopers: a basic sleeve, bodice, shift dress, princess-line dress, jacket, pant, and skirt pattern. From these basic fitted pieces, using
(continues on page 24)

This dress pieced from semi-sheer and lightweight nude and cream tones reveals the shape of each pattern piece, carefully formed to create this silhouette and follow the body's contours. Seams are curved, and subtle color differences in exquisite fabrics emphasize the design and craftsmanship of each panel.

FRANCISCO COSTA, FOR
CALVIN KLEIN,
Minas, Brazil/New York, NY, USA

Sonia Rykiel's ribbed, heathered knit sculpts the body softly and comfortably into a tailored suit shape for a woman's needs. The front has slight shaping into the waist seam, but the silhouette is really defined in back by a peplum waist and vertical seaming releasing into swaying flares below the derriere. A warm roll of functional collar builds the shape beautifully.

WWW.SHUTTERSTOCK.COM

Sonia Rykiel

PARIS

"A bag on her shoulder and a child in each hand," according to Sonia Rykiel, is the Rykiel woman.

Sonia Rykiel was born May 25, 1930, Russian-Romanian Jewish, the eldest of five daughters, in Neuilly, France. She has had retrospective exhibits and is known as a successor to Chanel for her simple, innovative, modern, and feminine fashions. A self-declared "universal women's designer," she addresses work, dreams, and family life in her designs.

Known as the Queen of Knits in the United States, she, to this day, does *not* know how to knit. Jean Paul Gaultier is known to tease her for this. Rykiel fell into fashion design (and, ironically, says she spent the first ten years trying to get out of it) when she became pregnant and wanted to be "the most beautiful pregnant woman."

She had married the owner of a French boutique called Laura and started designing knitwear when she couldn't find any fashionable maternity clothes. She used one of her husband's knit suppliers to produce her first pieces and continued designing for the well-to-do French women who shopped at Laura through the 1960s. Rykiel started to build a following in the United States, known for her "poor boy" sweater and skinny knits in neutral, muted colors and striped patterns (although she prefers to wear black herself).

She has been quoted saying that she couldn't relate to the first fashion she made, even though it was fashion . . . it didn't relate to her life, the life of a woman, mother, and worker, and that she envisioned her woman surrounded by "bags and children," busy, out and about. (She has two children of her own.) This is what guided her work, along with her professed value of "seduc-

tion." Her passionate singularity of vision has been the foundation of her success. Rykiel wanted to "undo" fashion until it would meet her life: clothes that traveled, stacked, reversed, transformed from day into eveningwear. One of the first deconstructionists, she started putting the seam allowances on the outside. She was also an early proponent of "high-low" fashion, mixing the expensive with the inexpensive. In the 1990s, she designed in a range of fabrics, including crepes, tweeds, velvets—all popular with the body-conscious, gym-toned bodies of the era. Her clingy knits are combined with loose, boxy, and flowing pieces. She has designed two casual collections per year since the 1980s, consisting of a dress, trousers, pullovers, cardigans, and jackets combining to create clean silhouettes.

Rykiel has authored many books and considers herself "more of an author than designer" who writes a "new chapter" each season, based on the life she sees around her. Also, it is common to see English or French words blazoned across her garments, such as *Plaisir* (pleasure), Artist, or often her own name.

Her Boulevard de St. Germain lifestyle boutique opened in 1990, and her first Paris boutique celebrated its forty-year anniversary in 2008. Today, she works hand-in-hand with her daughter Nathalie, who also maintains that no matter how many people are helping, she needs to be at the center of her business for it to succeed.

These garments feature a squared, built-up sleeve cap and collar shape. Armhole and neckline seams are replaced with a single over-arm/shoulder seam shaped at the collar, shoulder, and sleeve hem for a distinctive, clear silhouette.

BASHARATYAN V,
BY VERONICA BASHARATYAN,
London, UK/Moscow, Russia

a traditional dressmaker's approach, new pattern shapes can be created, controlling the actual shaping of each seam or panel, and thus, the shape of the finished garment.

Pattern shapes can be combined to create new shapes. For example the sleeve can be morphed with the bodice to create a one-piece front and back if the armscye is dropped and the shoulder seam extends all the way to the wrist, as in a dolman, batwing, or kimono sleeve. This gives a line that can be manipulated and shaped, adding or subtracting volume to the designer's will (if the fabric cooperates) to create a whole range of silhouettes.

Strong overall triangular form with soft, flared finish at the hem balances angles with curves. The secondary shape story is the full-circular cut of the cape, over a minuscule pattern of circular snaps trailing down the pants leg, and square belt buckle.

ELENA GOLETS,
Kiev, Ukraine

Sketchbook. These sketches show variations on a blocking-only theme using lines, angles, and panels to create an evening group with widely varied silhouettes. The shape of individual garment panels is explored as much as how they relate to the overall shape.

TOMMY TA,
New York, NY, USA

In another example, the sleeve can cut into part of the bodice, creating a raglan line that can extend into a shaped stand-up neckline in-one with the bodice. Similarly, a two-piece jacket-sleeve cut has many more shaping options than a sleeve with only one seam. A basic straight skirt can be slashed and opened at the hem to create an A-line, flared, or full-circle skirt. If volume or length is added to only one side of the pattern, the result will be asymmetrical shape.

Necklines, armholes, hemlines, and princess seams (vertical seams dividing a garment into usually fitted panels) all are vulnerable to the designer's vision and are

Using a single, solid, and firm fabric with classic dressmaker details emphasizes the importance of the overall shape reminiscent of the fifties: fitted bodice, darts and pleats, full skirt, cap sleeve, and belted waist for nostalgic elegance. The expert fit lends its shape to the body inhabiting it.

BARBARA TFANK,
New York, NY, USA

The basic shift-dress pattern, anchored to the right shoulder, is slashed and opened down the left side seam, adding godets of fabric excess, which are then lifted and tacked (stitched with right sides together to expose 4 inches [10.2 cm] of seam allowance falling outside). All in richly colored silk, the basic shift's shape is retained but with all of that added weight. The shoulder seam also joins in the flow.

ALLDRESSEDUP,
BY TINA TAN-LEO,
Singapore, Malaysia

able to take on the specific cut-out shapes desired. Alexander McQueen, Francisco Costa, Byron Lars, and Thierry Mugler are some masters of shaped seaming exploration. Patch pockets, pocket flaps, collars, lapels, belts, yokes, and waistbands are other garment foundations that can be bent and twisted into any shape that can be imagined, while still retaining the use they were intended for.

Prints, patterns, and textures are the more minute carriers of shapes, but when used this way, shape remains two-dimensional.

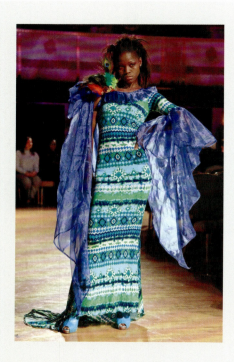

A straight, raglan-sleeved column dress has a busy geometric print (microshapes arranged in horizontal rows) that takes center stage. Its shape is punctuated by a wide, contrast-pleated neckline ruffle and floor-length, circular flared sleeve ruffles with square hems.

OUCH COUTURE
BY UCHE NNEJI,
Lagos, Nigeria

Shaped edges are explored using solid colors for clarity, whether in soft silk or firm gilded woven fabric. Asymmetry through overlap is part of the theme.

DEVOTA Y LOMBA,
BY MODESTO LOMBA.
Madrid, Spain

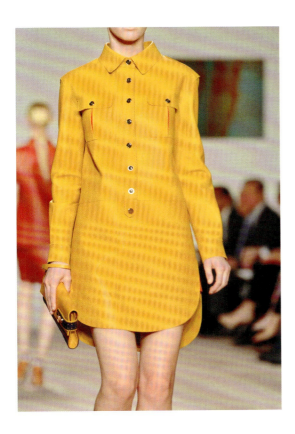

The clean-cornered collar and shoulders and shirt-sleeve cuffs in this shirtdress pull maximum drama by contrasting with rounded shirttails elegantly, softening the A-line silhouette.

TOMMY HILFIGER,
New York, NY, USA

sil·hou·ette \ sil-oo-et \ *n*
1: the outline or general shape
of something

3

Though often represented from the front, any sculptor will remind you that fashion, as with any three-dimensional form, should be considered from every angle. Garments are often cut as a front and a back, joined at the side seam, but side

seams are not essential, and wrapping the body and seaming in other areas can explore draping as an escape from cookie-cutter shaping of garments with matching front and back silhouettes.

In early civilization, garments weren't cut so much. A sari wraps the body with no cuts. Kimonos, caftans, sarouels, ponchos, and tunics are minimally cut to preserve precious handwoven or patterned fabric. The exact proportions of the fabric pieces in relation to the body, combined with the fabric's weight or texture, always result in its silhouette: pure shape and its immediate impact.

(continues on page 32)

Potentially a wedding piece, this pure white, straight silhouette is punctuated by an extravagant exposed bustle of gathered ruffles that diminishes the waist, emphasizes the small of the back, lifts the eye (usually gravity pulls fullness to the hem), and echoes and amplifies the rounded protrusion of the heel. Frivolous and feminine, it brings back the drama of the peplum and carefully considers the profile silhouette. Dangling ties add movement.

BOUDDICCA,
BY ZOWIE BROACH AND
BRIAN KIRBY,
London, UK

Betsey Johnson

NEW YORK

Always looking ahead and behind in fashion, but always outside of trends and inside her heart, Betsey Johnson was one of the very first emphasizing street fashion as inspiration for her line. She also pioneered the use of fabrics with specific associations, such as baseball striping, car upholstery fabric, and shower curtains—taken out of context for her designs. Her personal style with red lipstick and radical, brightly cut geometric hair is an iconic fashion in itself. Joy and life are the first ingredients in the Betsey Johnson experience.

Betsey Johnson, born in 1942, grew up in Connecticut and graduated magna cum laude from Syracuse University in 1964. She came to New York with no connections or knowledge about the fashion business. A guest editor stint at *Mademoiselle* magazine landed her a permanent position in their art department, which sent her to London in the age of the Beatles and bell-bottoms and Carnaby Street fashion. She fell in love.

She first appeared on the New York fashion scene designing outrageous styles for a boutique called Paraphernalia. She revolutionized American fashion with space-age silver and see-through plastic dresses, and a dress with a noisy metal grommeted hem, elephant bell-bottoms, and micro minis.

She first made her name opening her own boutique, Betsey Bunki Nini, in downtown Manhattan before launching her Betsey Johnson boutiques. She says she still does very much the same things she always did, that fashion doesn't change all that much, and that she is not a fashion designer as much as someone who loves to make things. ("I just have to make things.")

Her daughter Lulu is her top print and runway model. She also draws from her background in dance and her body type (small top, large bottom—she's her own fit model) when designing. She aims to fill a niche for special, fun, dreamy clothing for every woman's closet. Her clothes have always been reasonably priced and drawn from youth culture: British American invasion, punk, deconstruction, rave, gothic, grunge, and ballerina, to name a few. Movie stars, musicians, and models have all sported her unique looks.

After becoming free of breast cancer, she is involved in raising awareness and funds for the cause. She is one of the twenty-eight American designers honored on Fashion's Walk of Fame on Seventh Avenue. In order to stay profitable in hard times, she closed her boutiques in 2012 to sell exclusively online. Her work is as current and hip now as it ever was, as is she.

Silhouette is in clear focus in this group. Crisp, stable shapes in natural fiber, medium-weight fabrics are constructed with classic dressmaking techniques for uncommon results. Volumes and space are built between the body and the garment's outside edge in architectural forms. Add some fluid fabrics for asymmetry and rethink basic silhouettes with fitted waists, prominent shoulders, and uneven hemlines. The shape achieved appears to be the guiding focus of the group. Headgear is an important component of the overall shape.

ANNE BORELLI,
*Rio de Janeiro, Brazil/
Miami, FL, USA*

A garment's unique silhouette personality takes on a life of its own, whether on a human, a hanger, or a display table.

Fashion begins with a body. We wrap it in fabric, enclose it in a garment, and get instant impact. A garment's size and the character of its shape are registered at a glance. That is silhouette. Details such as nuances of contours and edges become visible next. Imagine a stark black shape against a white background for an immediate mental image of silhouette.

Tuning in to silhouette in favor of details for a moment gives the designer, illustrator, or wearer precise control over the aesthetics of shape.

This softly woolen coatdress is 100 percent silhouette, fused with color and absolutely no distractions. Smooth and minimal, narrow shoulders and a collar cut in-one with the bodice blend into an above-bust dart for a semifitted waist. An armhole is replaced with an overarm seam to shape the one-piece bodice/sleeve. A simple waist seam and hidden closures widen to a floor-length, elegant A-line.

JESUS DEL POZO,
Madrid, Spain

Note that a fashion silhouette is never defined by garment alone—the hairstyle, body, shoes, mix of garment pieces, and accessories all contribute greatly to the final shape and effect, and the story becomes more complex and new looks are created as shapes play off one another.

The relative proportions of the parts in a look result in the silhouette. Some of the most common components defining a look are the waistline and the location of its definition (high, low, natural) or lack thereof; hips (high or low, emphasized or deemphasized); collars (built up, wide or close to the neck, voluminous, or flat); sleeves (full, narrow, belled, puffed); neckline widths and depths; and bust shaping. Pants may have rounded or creased hems, wide or fitted legs, draped or flat fronts and backs. Skirts vary in lengths, hems, and localized fullness. Garment and body silhouettes may be characterized as triangle, square, inverted triangle, trapeze, boxy, hourglass, fitted, pear shaped, pencil, cocoon, trumpet, flute, pouf, and mermaid, and so on.

Since the edge of the garment shape reflects the character of the fabric used in that garment (fur, leather, chiffon, batiste, tweed, nylon, neoprene, cashmere jersey,

Masterful construction in neutral-colored luxury fabrics builds crisp, decisive silhouette shapes that urge to be viewed from every angle. The wide, flat hair silhouettes play into the narrow and wide stories of each look, as do the high platform shoes.

FLYNOW, BY CHAMNAN PAKDISUK,
Bangkok, Thailand

Solid color used to draw attention to a carefully sculpted shape based on the female form fused with tailored suiting details. Built-up shoulders, fitted waist, and an exaggerated hip with pocket excess do the job. Adding width to the hip and shoulder creates the illusion of a tiny waist by comparison.

ALINA ASSI,
Moscow, Russia

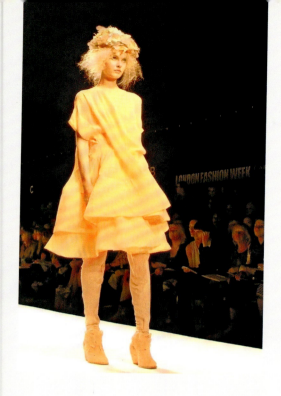

Knowing how fabrics and cuts behave paves the way for exploring and bringing fresh ideas to silhouette, without clinging to the body's shape for security. These fabrics are capable of holding width without weighing down through innovative cuts and drapes taking on a precious shape of their own, topped off with a fantastic bonnet.

JOHN ROCHA,
Hong Kong/Ireland

canvas, etc.), every garment's fabrication weight and surface texture is expressed in a silhouette, naturally, based on its behavior as manipulated by the designer's intention.

Pattern has no effect on silhouette, while texture defines the contours of the garment. Fabric weight, garment structure and infrastructure, as well as edge-finishing techniques are used to build up or diminish areas in the silhouette. Absence of color blocking, rich texture, pattern, or other distractions will, in fact, make the pure silhouette's impact the first element noticed in a look. For this purpose, I have used primarily solid looks to illustrate this principle.

These pants have a fitted ankle and waistband, while everything else is extended and minimally constructed with maximum fabric. When released, deep cowls will form on the sides. The silhouette of the garment in the model's hands is quite different than when it succumbs to gravity. The crotch and inseam length has to be designed long enough to allow the legs to stride.

IN-PROCESS,
BY HALL OHARA,
Tokyo, Japan

line \ ˈlīn \ *n*

1: a mark or stroke long in proportion to its breadth, made with a pen, pencil, tool, etc., on a surface.

4

Stripes, strips, and straps. Princess line, waistline, seam line, hemline, and A-line. Yarn, thread, pencil, and brush. Line quality. Timelines, deadlines, designing, producing, presenting a line of clothing. What isn't linear about fashion? Garments are cut

FIRSTVIEW.COM

from lines that wrap themselves around the human form, surrounding it, while fabric is woven from them.

Each thread, seam, and row of knitting is a line. Spaghetti straps, leather belts, gold chains, ribbons, zipper tape, arms, and legs all take on linear forms that can twist, bend, surround, follow, border, crease, ruche, slash, but somehow remain lines. Lines are the result of edges meeting; they carry the eye through time and space, marking separations, taking us on a journey, wrapping, fitting, enveloping the human form. Lines can intersect. (continued on page 41)

Over a clean-lined bias slip top in linen, burnished, rippling leather is integrated in contrast, wrapping the neck and splitting the garment with an overlapping intersection of forms.

ANIMALE,
BY KARLLA GIROTTO,
São Paulo, Brazil

Vera Wang

NEW YORK

Vera Wang was raised on Manhattan's affluent Upper West Side. When she was seven, she was gifted a pair of ice skates and began a career of skating and competing through her twenties. When she didn't make it into the U.S. Olympic team, she decided to change careers, and clothing was the only thing she loved as much as skating. She started working for *Vogue* magazine, bringing with her the professionalism and finish she acquired in her skating career, and was promoted to fashion editor after her first year. She stayed there for sixteen years, until a new editor in chief was appointed.

She then became a design director for sixteen accessories lines at Ralph Lauren. In 1989, she was frustrated by her search for a wedding dress at age forty, feeling that dresses dictated too much to young women, and she wanted something more personal. She designed two of her own and hired a dressmaker to make them. She knew she could bring something special back to weddings, giving women more than the bridal market was offering, dresses that suited their personalities rather than "putting on a dress" that dictates to the wearer. In 1990, she opened her bridal boutique on Madison Avenue, carrying well-known designers as well as her own designs.

She says that when she designs, she really tries to think about what the garment is supposed to accomplish. Whether it is romance, sexiness, or modernity, she saw how she could satisfy the needs of the contemporary bride and revive the art of bridal design. Her styles became known for being luxurious, classic, simple, beautiful, and couture-like in style. She doesn't work only by sketch, but by holding and sculpting fabric and washing, testing, experimenting with, and developing fabrics and finishes.

Design and skating came together again when she designed Nancy Kerrigan's skating costumes for the Olympics. Made-to-order and ready-to-wear pieces by Wang, bridal and otherwise, are sought by celebrities and carried by top boutiques and retailers like Bergdorf Goodman and Saks Fifth Avenue. She also designs lines for Kohl's and David's Bridal, mass retailers, bringing her experience and aesthetic to women who could not afford her pieces otherwise. Working on many lines for many functions cross-fertilizes and inspires her work on each line. Now with many lines, including ready-to-wear and mass-market collaborations for different price points, she admits that four times a year is a grueling schedule for staying creative and fresh in the fashion business, but she manages.

Understanding the importance of celebrity dressing has certainly boosted her visibility and business success. She moved naturally into eveningwear from bridal with a philosophy that strives to be sophisticated without looking costumed. Another successful designer who designs for herself, she values comfort with enough structure to support and accentuate the positive and gentle draping to skim over the rest. She wants women who wear her clothes to feel secure and sexy.

Technical drawing of military jacket. Using waterproof felt pens, varied line weights, and colors clarifies specific information such as stitch type, seams, lapped edges, drawstring tunnel, pockets, and topstitching details.

ROXANE GILBEY,
Sydney, Australia

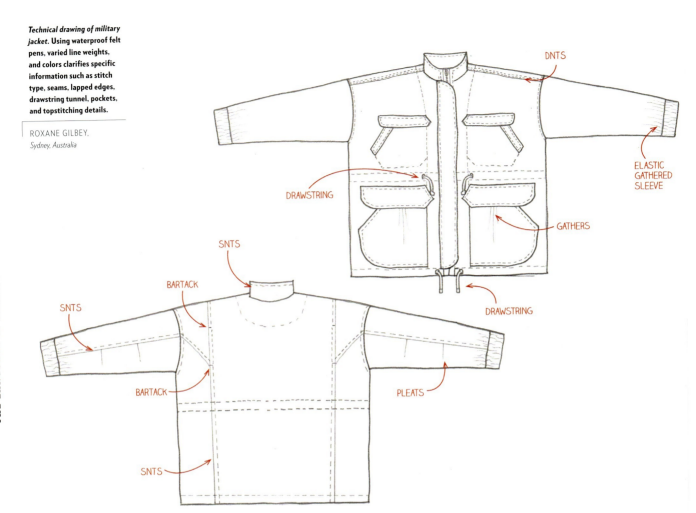

DNTS

ELASTIC GATHERED SLEEVE

DRAWSTRING

GATHERS

DRAWSTRING

SNTS

BARTACK

SNTS

BARTACK

SNTS

PLEATS

Every facet of these masterful garments is translated
into line and plane. The pattern pieces will reflect curved
aspects, but the seams and
edges emphasize angles as
seen on the body, and precise
pressing makes each shape
stand to attention.

DUSK TIL DAWN,
BY NISSARA
LIPTAWATTANA,
Bangkok, Thailand

Overlap of line translates visually as layers
in space. (When lines interrupt each other,
one becomes visually forward, the other falls
behind in space.) The higher the contrast
in drawn line from dark to light and thick to
thin, the more dramatic its impact.

In technical drawings and illustrations,
a variety of line weights prioritize information for the viewer, making images easier to
understand. Any image that uses only one
weight of line will call the eye to every line at
the same time, but also have a spatially flat-
tening effect. This can be desirable, too, for
certain stylistic applications, so experience
and awareness are important.

**Sketchbook detail, illustra-
tion. Quick pencil sketches
articulate ideas to life for
the design of a collection.
Flares, seams, necklines,
armholes, figures, and legs
in a variety of weights create
spatial depth; flowing lines
create movement and life on
the page. Illustration with
gouache features linear-** **based design concepts in
proportions, pose, edges,
and seams.**

ADENIYI OKWUBOYEJO,
Nigeria/New York, NY, USA

A crisp, clean minimalist trench has a clean-finished neckline, echoed by the capelet's curvilinear hem. Three horizontal lines follow, set off by deep shadows: the pocket flap; the square, free-floating pocket bag; and the skirt hem. Each narrower than the last, they express a slightly inverted triangle silhouette.

FERNANDO LEMONIEZ,
Madrid, Spain

Varied line weight adds excitement and intrigue, yet is more soothing to view than a consistently hard edge.

In fashion drawing, line quality is a hefty communication tool. Line quality refers to the dynamics (dark, light, thin, thick) of the drawn line or perceived edge. Variety of line occurs everywhere in nature and can also be observed in the corners, textures, grains, and edges of different fabric qualities in fashion. Line sketching is one of the most common ways to convey ideas. Claire Mc-Cardell's sketchbooks archived at Parsons' Gimbel Library are full of very simple pencil line drawings.

Drawn lines can be gritty, wet, precise, soft, harsh, rough, opaque, sheer, or technical in appearance. Line is what slashes pattern pieces, carves silhouettes, surrounds bodies, and cuts hems. Lines can be ribs or pleats; drawn by pencil, hand stitched, or topstitched; or they can be seamed panels. Even without trying, lines present themselves wherever edges meet—between figure and background or lapel and collar.

Layers, tiers, collars, openings, hems, and borders result in lines. Overlapping pieces will reveal themselves in line, and every line will have a unique quality.

Hair textures and styles, fur, lofty woolens, quilted fabrics, fluid silks, crisp pressed cottons, stand-out tulle, draped jersey, skintight Lycra, weighted leather—all materials in fashion present a unique kind of edge in the outlines of a garment. Illustrators are well versed in communicating these subtle differences of contour edges in lines, hems, and corners when creating fashion illustrations.

Pure white and pure linear detail decisively build a fitted jacket silhouette that is totally exposed, meticulous, and confident in its construction, execution, and seaming. Linear triads at the sleeve cuff create a pattern.

ANDREW GN,
Singapore/Paris, France

The shimmering liquid gown is dazzling with emphasized linear embellishment, dramatically lengthening from the heart to the floor. The deep V-neck is the focal point, with diagonal lines radiating gracefully toward the shoulders, high hip, and bust level. Sleeve hems are additional dashes.

NAEEM KHAN,
Mumbai, India/New York, NY, USA

bi·as \ ˈbaɪəs \ *n*

2: (Clothing, Personal Arts & Crafts/ Knitting & Sewing) a diagonal line or cut across the weave of a fabric.

5

In general, garments are cut with the length grain (parallel to the selvage edges of the raw material) running down the length of the piece. Called straight grain, it is stable and strong, its threads falling flat in the gridlike formation that weaving

naturally takes on a loom, resulting in crisp forms with square corners, and no horizontal or vertical stretch.

The development of the bias-cut technique is likened to the first action of deconstruction: It provoked a total rethinking of the medium. When a garment is cut diagonally from the cloth, or draped at a 45-degree rotation, woven threads take on a lattice formation rather than a grid, such that a square stretched horizontally becomes short and wide, or vertically becomes long and narrow. Bias makes woven fabric flexible without adding elastic fibers.

(continued on page 48)

A bias top and skirt behave differently due to dramatically different textures, but note how gentle the diagonal lines are on the body, both through the gently draped top and the sequin-coated skirt. In both cases, it is free to move and unconstrained by the use of bias.

VENEXIANA,
BY KATI STERN,
Venice, Italy

Monique Lhuillier

LOS ANGELES

Monique Lhuillier was born in Cebu City, Philippines, in 1971, to a Vietnam-born French businessman and a former model of Spanish descent. She was exposed to fashion design at a young age, with her mother making clothes and running a small business out of their home, and black was forbidden as a clothing color option to Lhuillier and her siblings as teens. As a young woman, Lhuillier would work with local couturiers sketching out ideas to design her own dresses to wear to social events. She graduated from FIDM (Fashion Institute of Design and Merchandising) in 1995 and started working at Melivier, a bridal company, but found she wanted a more creative outlet.

When she became engaged, she felt restricted by the choices of bridalwear that made her feel dowdy and overly decorated. While she did find a dress to purchase, she designed all the wedding party's twenty-five dresses herself. When the wedding was over, there were business cards waiting for her at the desk of the Ritz-Carlton where the wedding party was held. With a $20,000 loan from her parents, she designed five wedding gowns and some bridesmaid's dresses and rented a booth at a bridal trade show, which she left with five new accounts, and her business was born.

She founded Monique Lhuillier and Company with her husband, Tom Bugbee, in 1996, as a bridal couturier based in Los Angeles. She began designing her own gowns in 2001, opening a Beverly Hills retail store. She then launched a ready-to-wear line in 2003, at New York Fashion Week, the same year that she was invited to join the Council of Fashion Designers of America (CFDA). She is renowned for her red-carpet dresses and romantic evening gowns as well as her bridal and bridesmaid's designs. Her philosophy is pared down. She doesn't believe in overaccessorizing or detailing—she believes that the woman should shine before the dress. Her language is feminine, expressed in the materials, trimmings, and forms of her bridal beginnings, but she is exploring and broadening her range in ready-to-wear with increasingly edgy silhouettes, patterns, and shapes.

This is a textbook-perfect example of a bias gown's drape and fit in silk charmeuse. All seams and edges use the straight grain, because it's easily controllable. They all hit the figure at 45-degree angles, including the clever negative-shaped diamonds plus pendants at center front.

DONA DANESHI,
Persia/Los Angeles, CA, USA

A new orientation can be achieved by rotating the material 45 degrees from the straight grain, called the true bias. Fabric on bias can be used for its diagonal surface pattern or for its unique structural effects. Either way, using bias instead of straight grain will change a fabric's behavior as it falls along the body, and depending on how it's folded or finished. What would be a crisp or linear piece with the length grain running straight down it becomes rounded, moldable, and flexible on bias. Madeleine Vionnet, Madame "Alix" Grès, Claire McCardell, and Halston are some of the pioneers of the bias cuts now used by so many designers.

FIRSTVIEW.COM

A straight-cut top and sleeves and bias-cut skirt complement each other. The shift in the skirt's pattern makes the bias obvious, as is the change in the fabric's behavior as the skirt extends itself completely smooth over the hip, lending a precise fit, then releasing into flares where the stretching ends.

DURO OLOWU,
Nigeria/London, UK

Bias can also create challenges. Laying out pattern pieces obliquely will take up more space across its width (usually 44 or 60 inches [1.1 to 1.5 m]), and thus may require joined panels to completely cut the garment's silhouette within the fabric's borders. These seams will have to be incorporated into the design.

Stitching through the bias will naturally cause an edge to stretch and ripple, which can be desirable or problematic depending on the desired effect. For example, bias is wonderful for a lettuce-leaf ripple effect on a hem, but disastrous on the cut-out shape of a rounded neckline edge as it stretches prompltly out of shape. A stay or strip of

Chiffon empire trapeze is stitched through the true bias to create "lettuce leaf" ruffles in one with the skirt at the hem. The bias ruffles at the empire waist are inserted into the seam that holds the circle skirt.

MARIA BONITA EXTRA,
BY ANA MAGALHÃES,
Rio de Janeiro, Brazil

Straight-grain bodice construction in windowpane plaid is belted and relieved by bias-cut puffed sleeve caps pleated into the armhole, keeping the crisp bodice from looking too rigid, and a bias-cut necktie with an angled hem cooperates. Structural aspects aside, the plaid looks beautiful this way, and the mismatching of the plaid at the seams is not obvious as it would be with straight orientation.

MARC JACOBS,
New York, NY, USA

A true bias cut has infinite give through the lattice like orientation of its threads, adjusting themselves to fit by expanding horizontally while the garment becomes shorter. This expansive quality is used to accommodate a pregnant form without restriction, while draping flexibly into the sculpted folds at the shoulder.

UNKNOWN DESIGNER

Straight-grain bands of woven fabric are diagonally laid upon the figure, creating a handmade stripe, joining the visual and structural aspects of bias cutting. The solid sleeve on each piece is an interesting contrast detail.

AGATHA RUIZ
DE LA PRADA,
Madrid, Spain

It is easy to spot bias when a plaid is turned on its side. A loose yarn-dyed plaid drapes across the bodice as a textural layering piece.

CELIA VELA,
Figueres, Spain

woven fabric can help control the bias in such areas. Likewise, bands or strips of bias fabric are so flexible that they can be used for binding curved edges, for seam allowances like the Hong Kong finish, for facing curves, or for creating spaghetti tubing and cording. Also, true bias and edges cut on the bias do not unravel, because the threads at their edge hold an X shape.

Woven stripes or plaids always expose a garment's grain orientation because they make the grain visible. Even knit jersey naturally constructs its stripes horizontally across fabric width. These patterns offer a useful clue to recognizing the location and behavior of the bias grain and result in interesting geometric play combined with fluidity. Claire McCardell's garments are delightful to study in this way because of her common and creative use of plaid and stripe on bias.

An abundance of draped cowls lends opacity to a transparent top; the rounded rows of volume take the true bias straight down the center front line.

MARINA OBRADOVIC,
Zagreb, Croatia

block \ bläk \ *n*

1: A large, solid piece of material; typically with flat surfaces on each side.

6

Garments can be cut simply from flat square panels or shaped pieces. Such construction can be made almost invisible with carefully pressed, stitched seams in solid colors but can be made much more obvious by cutting each piece of the

garment in a different fabric or coloration. So blocking can happen within a garment or by mixing different solid-colored garments into a multicolored overall look. This common practice is called blocking, color blocking, or fabric blocking, with divisions between the different pieces made obvious by their contrast. This is also a way to construct line, because wherever edges meet, a line is created.

Color blocking or fabric blocking within a garment can bring together a whole fabric or color story onto a single jacket, skirt, or blouse, for a rich visual or textural effect.

(continued on page 57)

Horizontal and vertical edges are created where sundrenched, emotive colors are cut and sewn together to create new maxi patterns. Solid panels and bands of fabric seem to create oversized motifs and shapes that take over the body with volume, color, and direction, as if they were cut from magnificently **huge patterned fabrics instead of pieced together from individual bolts.**

AGATHA RUIZ
DE LA PRADA,
Madrid, Spain

Tracy Reese

NEW YORK

Tracy Reese, born in 1964, is a native of Detroit. Her bright, eclectic use of color and print is unique and lively. Her superfeminine dresses are both modern and nostalgic, full of dressmaker details. Philosophically, she doesn't believe in creating pieces just to "fill in" a collection of separates or just to go with a certain jacket or skirt. She maintains that every piece in the group should be able to stand alone on its design integrity. Reese says her pieces embrace women of different shapes, sizes, and colors and are not basics nor classics, but "hopefully essentials," and that she would never design anything that she wouldn't wear herself.

When she was growing up, her mother was a modern dance instructor and head of a high school art department who made a point of exposing her daughters to the arts. The women in her family who sewed would have contests to see who could finish making an outfit first.

Reese went to Parsons School of Design in New York on a summer scholarship, loved it, and enrolled full-time in 1982. She apprenticed with Martine Sitbon in New York after graduation and was assigned to her Arlequin line.

Reese worked at top fashion houses in New York, including Perry Ellis Portfolio, where she was womenswear design director, and her former classmate, Marc Jacobs, was president. In the early nineties, she became head designer at Magaschoni, a bridge line owned by the producers of Calvin Klein and Donna Karan. She was so successful that they gave her her own line, Tracy Reese for Magaschoni.

She eventually started her own label, presenting a modern woman in feminine, modern yet nostalgic luxury clothing. In 1998, she launched a second line, Plenty, which was more bohemian and ethnic in inspiration. Working with fabric manufacturers and hands in India, this more adventurous line still has Reese's signature details and lasting, not trendy, styles. She says that after twenty-five years in the business, she is still amazed by how she can create a print—especially in the digital age—out of anything. As a buyer once told her, a print can be the "road map" for a collection, leading the way. By 2002, she established her New York showroom. Her resort and swimwear lines, along with a party dress line called Frock!, are all based on her core values: delivering a quality garment that serves the woman at a fair price. She opened her New York Tracy Reese flagship store in downtown Manhattan in 2006, carrying all of her apparel lines, accessories, and home goods. She was inducted to the board of the CFDA in 2007 and is worn by Michelle Obama. In 2011, she opened a Tokyo store.

Subtle color blocking plays out in a variety of ways in Reese's collections. Textural and color blocking of layered pieces within a collection emphasizes the negative shapes between pieces. Blocking patterns, prints, or colors within an individual piece combines interesting fabrics and highlights construction lines.

Croquis book. Whether bright or subdued, Virgen's distinct style boldly works out shapes in blocked color either within the piece or within the look, with an excellent sense of balance across the collection. These are quick sketches in gouache.

PAULINA VIRGEN,
Calexico, CA, USA

This color-blocked skirt doesn't repeat any fabric. Each vertical, uniquely colored silk panel is shaped from a fitted waist to a full hem, lengthening the silhouette visually, and each block is bordered with rich metallic trim. It's all sealed together with two more blocks, actually bands of color at the hem, also carrying a metallic motif.

ANURADHAA BISANI,
Chennai, India

Mixing woven with knit within a single garment, for example, can also be exciting and add comfort where it is needed, such as in a tailored jacket with knitted sleeves. Blocking can be a way to mix textures on a piece. Style lines can be added into a garment simply for the aesthetic joy of attaching different fabrics to one another, or necessary fit lines can be used to bring contrasting panels together.

Color blocking can also create optical illusions, playing on the brain's impulse to group like objects together by color, so that separate garments or components can appear joined rather than separate simply because of their association by color. Likewise, one garment can be broken down into visible pieces by using contrasting colored pieces.

Classic solid pieces are merchandised to be worn in a color-blocked play of vibrant lengths and layers of gorgeous fabric qualities.

RACHEL ZOE,
Los Angeles, CA, USA

The simple division of silky knife pleats into two different dusty tones at center front is quietly interesting on the skirt, creating visual asymmetry along the center in line with the vertical pleats. Countered by a block of bias-draped cowls, the skirt silhouette is invaded by horizontal arcs. All fabrics are fluid, but curves and lines are separated by color. The darkest block at the waistline diminishes the waist among wide shoulders and hem.

KINA FERNANDEZ,
Madrid, Spain

Color blocking yields asymmetry strictly through the placement of color. In a Mondrian-esque composition of framed primary hues, the in-seam pocket is improvised to create width at the hip. Neckline, waist, and bust are delineated with rounded black bars, but the hip line is pronounced only by the ruler-straight pocket edges over a curved hem. All of this hinges on one glittering gold exposed zipper front in a very deliberate design.

DASHA GAUSER,
Moscow, Russia

Red blouse and white trousers unite to create a single visual block of color and "erase" the fly-front closure, waistband, and crotch seam from the focus of classic trousers, blending to create the illusion of an inverted, teardrop-shaped hem. The printed jacket creates a third block of softer, darker color that appears almost as a transparent layer of fine, rhythmic pattern.

CHRISTIAN COTA,
Mexico City, Mexico/
New York, NY, USA

Straight lines or curves can be created by joining fabric panels, either in complex, laborious patchworks or minimal piecing. Even a monochromatic look can be texturally blocked or blocked into varying levels of opacity or tones. Blocking plays on a garment's constuction and the human perception's tendency to group like items.

con·struc·tion \ kuhn-struhk-shuhn \ *n*
1: the act or art of constructing. **2:** the
way in which a thing is constructed.

7

construction

From haute couture, to traditional and ethnic, to modern-day mass-production methods, whether rendered invisible or exposed and obvious, construction, together with fabric and figure, provides the basis for the language of fashion. Industries,

60
61

and individuals like Isabel Toledo, have each developed a unique vocabulary of procedures and techniques for constructing clothes. The current industrial methods are called into question today as more sustainable and humane methods are sought for creating fashion and fabrics. Contemporary designers work within or outside current standard practices according to their vision. But all garments, as three-dimensional forms, involve a process of building.

Garments are generally built by bringing pieces of fabric together, using seams, ties, perhaps zippers, buttons, hooks, and so on. (continued on page 64)

Sheer organza reveals construction totally. Here, baby-hemmed circular flare ruffles follow all hemlines, seams, and openings, and fine 1/8-inch pin tucks punctuate the center front hip of the skirt, releasing into gentle fullness. A center-front button placket is classic.

CAROLINA HERRERA,
New York, NY, USA

FIRSTVIEW.COM

Isabel & Ruben Toledo

NEW YORK

Isabel and Ruben Toledo both immigrated to the United States from Cuba as children and met in high school. Their subsequent marriage produces their designs. Isabel humbly identifies herself as a seamstress (not a fashion designer), and Ruben as the artist/illustrator. Their design process is a never-ending dialogue: They tell each other what they are thinking and execute with each other's input. The result of this has been captured in years of sketchbooks. The couple declares that they are totally enmeshed artists, not because they think alike but, in fact, because they don't, and everything they make is born as a result of sharing their perspectives.

The Toledos show how success can be achieved by shaping their business as their art, keeping it small so that they can create freely. Both self-taught artists, they believe fashion must be original, must mean something, and encourage young designers to discover their own way of doing things.

Isabel learned to sew as a child when her mother enrolled her in a sewing class to keep her busy. She would alter her hand-me-down clothes, because she wanted to have control over how she looked. Later, while taking a ceramics class, throwing clay on the potter's wheel taught her the importance of working "in the round," which is now fundamental to her technique, draping on the mannequin and herself. When mentoring students, she stresses the importance of including a side view in their sketching process, which is often overlooked in schools.

She began restoring couture garments in the Metropolitan Museum's Costume Institute in New York for five years, and there she started to recognize fashion as an art form through its construction. Inside each historical and iconic garment, she could see how the pieces were built, thought out, and designed. Thus, she learned her construction techniques from the great designers and garments and maintains that how things are made is the art form. Most of her constructions and methods are nontraditional and experimental.

Isabel and Ruben gave biannual runway shows from 1984 through 1998, starting when she was twenty-five, but pulled out as the system became prohibitively expensive and fast for a designer who works so independently. Stressing the importance of process, she says that she always finishes an idea, and that ideas that don't work give birth to other ideas, so nothing is ever lost. For example, she will tell Ruben an idea, and if he sketches it wrong, it leads to other ideas. She insists that the personal journey of form is what develops the individual artist's language of making garments.

Isabel and Ruben, together, were awarded the 2005 Cooper-Hewitt National Design Award. In 2008, Isabel Toledo was presented with the third annual Couture Council Award for Artistry of Fashion from the Museum at FIT. Michelle Obama wore her ensemble for the inauguration in 2009, culminating Isabel's early observations that fashion is an expression of time, always marking its era.

Delicate, crisp organdy reveals construction with clarity. This dress seems to have been built right on the mannequin in classic Toledo style, with pin tucks at a paper-bag waist, a rippling band of variegated horizontal pleating embellishing the center front, and shaped darts in the fitted bodice. Tulle peeks from the hem.

The result is a textural, sculpted silhouette. Ruben's illustrations hover overhead.

The house of Calvin Klein's infamous minimalism constructs with as few lines as possible, drawing immediate attention first to the woman. The basic shapes are executed in highly developed fabric qualities that are designed to last. Razor-sharp lines, angles, and corners build the precise notched collar on a jacket.

CALVIN KLEIN COLLECTION, BY FRANCISCO COSTA
New York, NY, USA/Minas, Brazil

Finishes on cut edges and seams are a basic consideration of construction, lending comfort, beauty, and lasting durability. Fit and form are achieved with the basic vocabulary of gathers, pleats, and flares to add or subtract fullness where needed. Notions are the often-hidden secrets supporting the shape of a "built" garment. Designers can impose their will on a fabric's behavior by using interfacing, boning, horsehair braid, or tulle to add stiffness where needed; padding in the shoulders, bust, or hips to build silhouette; or lining to hide hand stitches and seam allowances. Snaps, elastic, twill tape, and seam binding aim to clean-finish, shape, squeeze,

Working with the fabric's character, a bias skirt is pleated into a fitted bodice. Obvious seams are decorative and add volume where desired at the same time.

DAVID TLALE,
Cape Town, South Africa

and control garment edges and panels to fit, flow, form, or finish. Other designers make a point of working more integrally and use only the fabric's inherent properties to create a shape.

Structured garments require precise fitting and engineering, but this doesn't always mean they are comfortable. Comfort is a modern part of fashion's goals, but as humans continue to use fashion to change or alter the appearance of their body shape, construction can still mean constriction as well.

The principal body measurements are in the bust, bicep, waist, thigh, and hip,

With halters, drawstrings, gathers, layered ruffles, flares, pin tucks, tiers, and zippers, these pieces are based on the elements of dressmaking to create fresh looks that effortlessly build shapes with volume. The absence of surface pattern draws attention to the construction.

JULIANA JABOUR,
*Belo Horizonte,
Minas, Brazil*

Visible seam lines follow the body in a fitted patchwork or create their own shape independent of the body's form.

GARETH PUGH,
London, UK

representing the maximum and minimum circumferences of the body.

Darts, gathers, pleats, flares, and other construction techniques are typically used to navigate the body's shape from these largest to smallest measurement requirements for comfort and aesthetic purposes. They can also be used independent of fit as controllers, to add and subtract volume and piece fabric panels together wherever desired in a garment, while simultaneously creating surface effects like ripples, folds, lines, curves, and ruffles. Seams, hem finishes, and other techniques used to put the garment together (and keep it that way) are functional necessities as well as areas for expression in a design.

In a single collection, masterful construction and deconstruction are intermingled. Clean, crisp, orderly seams and bows, bindings, and hand embellishments work alongside exposed darts, raw edges, pinking, and visible staystitching.

ALEXANDRE HERCHCOVITCH,
São Paulo, Brazil

How are pieces joined? New fabrics, technologies, and ingenious innovation can play on solutions to this question. Lacing and tying go back to origins. Hand stitching may be decorative, or invisible. Machine stitching and overlock/serging are standard. Nonwoven textiles may be heat melded or adhered to one another. Seamless garments are engineered for knitting machines.

The more detailed the construction, the more special the wearer may feel, and the more expensive the process of creating the precious piece. Complex piecing and many patterns show a richness and detail that the mass-produced eye is no longer used to seeing. Fine, detailed handwork will always be a sign of care, soul, and human skill. Simplification of construction processes can also be an expression of creativity, however. The pendulum may be swinging from ultra-cheap production methods to a more lasting fashion that involves less waste and values careful construction methods. Then again, who knows what technological innovations in construction lie ahead?

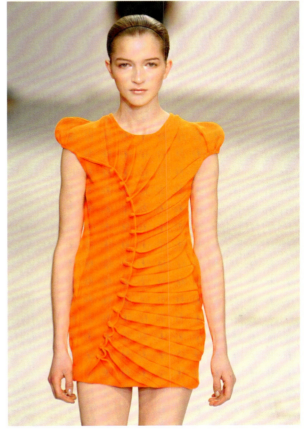

Expert manipulation of fabric creates a design on the surface, with a repetition of folds that surprises and amazes anyone who has struggled with manipulating fabrics in such a way. A solid-color base fabric calls full attention to the construction. The construction is the decoration.

AMAYA ARZUAGA,
Madrid, Spain/London, UK

drape \ drāp \ *vt*
1: to cover, surround, or hang with cloth or other fabric, esp. in graceful folds. **2:** to adjust (fabric, clothes, etc.) into graceful folds or attractive lines. **3:** to arrange, hang, or let fall carelessly. **4:** to hang, fall, or become arranged in folds, as drapery. *n.* **6:** manner or style of hanging

8

Fashion draping has two related meanings. Foremost, draping is known as the art and craft of taking fabric onto the body or the dress form/mannequin with scissors, pins, and pencil to cut, secure, slash, and mark the fabric to create a

unique garment form. Collars, sleeves, bodices, coats, or dresses can be draped freehand on a three-dimensional form, in muslin (which is inexpensive and easy to mark), orin the actual fabric (more expensive) to observe its behavior and observe its straight grain's orientation in relation to the garment's shape. During the draping process, seams are shaped by hand, exerting control over their quantity, angle, placement, and line. Draping the garment, a designer makes decisions working with the body's shape, the fabric's behavior, and the grain line. Often a (continued on page 72)

A straight-grain gown is fitted clean with vertical darts, while heavy cowls and drapery build up the shoulders in a fluid, rounded form.

ZANG TOI,
FOR HOUSE OF TOI
New York, NY, USA

GETTYIMAGES.COM

GETTYIMAGES.COM

Byron Lars

NEW YORK

Born in Oakland, California, in 1965, Byron Lars studied at the Brooks Fashion Institute, Long Beach, 1983–1985, and Fashion Institute of Technology, 1986–1987.

He participated in international fashion contests while in school, then freelanced in New York as a sketcher and pattern maker. At twenty-five, he decided it was time to sit down with his home sewing machine and make some samples, taking them to magazines and stores. Henri Bendel ordered forty pieces, and after he delivered them, he happily found them featured in the windows on Fifth Avenue. After only his second season in business, *Women's Wear Daily* hailed Lars as "Rookie of the Year."

Familiar pieces like classic white shirts and bomber jackets take on sensuously cut, Dior-esque, and forties-inspired yet contemporary silhouettes. His designs are classic yet edgy, sexy but never vulgar, superfeminine but menswear derived. Built-in bras, cinched waists and peplums, saronglike draping of shirting fabrics, and tying are hallmarks of Lars's approach. He took a classic men's shirt and morphed it into a sarong style. His wrapping and work with stripes and plaids are reminiscent of Claire McCardell, though his concepts are curvier and more fantastical, with lots of flourish.

His grandfather taught him that when edgy ideas are steeped in familiarity (the recognizable classic garment types that Lars uses), the consuming public accepts it more easily. Always bearing this in mind, his first-rate, ultrafeminine design and draping will start out as, for example, a hunting or baseball jacket that gets re-interpreted. The most iconic version of this is his hourglass interpretation of the bomber jacket, with racy seams and rugged construction that got so much press in the 1990s. But he is also known for his curvy, playful, overtly feminine, and expertly draped innovations on the classic white shirt. Reminiscent of Thierry Mugler or Azzedine Alaïa (contemporaries of his early career), his beautiful seaming builds fit and shape in a perfect marriage of function and form, with every construction detail artfully designed into a winding curve. His innovative construction shapes and lines are couturelike, truly outstanding and unique on the American design scene, mixing high fashion, street influence, and classic appropriations from menswear's forms and fabrics. The aesthetics and the approach to construction set him both above and apart as a designer.

In addition, he is known for theatrical and playful themes, personalities, and props in the presentation of his collections. Outrageous accessories that he had designed only as show props had licensees following him for the designs of hats, furs, and handbags. (Example: a duck decoy purse with the hunting jacket, which was later featured in a museum exhibit at FIT.)

After a licensing deal from 1995 to 1997 with his Shirttails line left him feeling that he had lost control over his line, he started again from scratch, with a new vision for how he wanted to do business. In 1999, he launched a line called Green T that didn't bear his name, so that he could focus on making great clothes without designer hype, at a great price. In 1996, Mattel invited him to create designer Barbie looks. This was the beginning of an ongoing relationship. First Lady Michelle Obama regularly attends events where his clothing is featured, and his current line is called Beauty Mark. Initially a cotton Lycra shirt-

ing–based offering, Beauty Mark took its cue from the shirts and shirtdresses of the previous collection that put the designer on the map at a more accessible price point. Since its inception ten years ago, his product line is now expanding to include knits, sportswear, and dresses, in addition to the chic and sexy shirts for which the line is sought after.

Creamy tones of matte and shiny, opaque and sheer ripples build flowery confections, each prettier than the next. Draped lengths, flared ruffle bands, fabric flowers, and fine finishes create asymmetrical gowns that are ostentatiously crafted with skill.

YOSAWADEE AND
BUSARDI,
Bangkok, Thailand

garment will be draped on half the mannequin, then traced over to create the other half, for symmetry.

When analyzing and discussing designs, drape refers to the lengths of fabric that are laid onto the body or into the garment. Whether a heavy swag of a cowl, or a smoothly cut-in dart following from the bust apex to the hip in a sheath dress, all are used to drape or lay the fabric length and secure it somehow to the body, and to itself. Darts, pleats, gathers, flares, shirring, and cowls are the fundamental vocabulary for securing quantities of fabric onto the human form. Darts or style lines cut away,

Maximum circular flare is draped into the waistline, while a vast volume is gathered across the bodice, secured by a band, and then released freely upward. Aesthetics and fit are combined.

HATTA DOLMAT,
Kuala Lumpur, Malaysia

subtracting from fabric volume, while the former techniques take lengths of volume and tack them down for subtle to dramatic effects. Pleats fold lengths into a seam or yoke, and gathers squeeze fabric into a small, secure edge. Flares are smooth at the seam line but wide at the free edge, resulting in conical abundance of fabric ripples. Cowls are collapsed (depending on the stiffness of the fabric) horizontal excesses that fall with gravity in a random shape.

Draping the raw material in every possible way is the designer's playground, manipulating and creating forms from the flat fabric. Innovative designers drape their own garments or rely on a team in studio to help them build shape into their garments.

It is easy to see the dart excess folded away behind each pleat in this shoulder seam and through the overarm seams of the full sleeves.

TATIANA PARFIONOVA,
Moscow, Russia

vol·ume \ ˈväl-yəm; -ˈyo͞om \ *n*
a: the amount of space occupied by a three-dimensional object or region of space. **b:** The capacity of such a region or container. **c:** Amount; quantity.

9

In fashion design, volume can refer to either the amount of fabric in a garment area or the amount of space it occupies. A lot of fabric doesn't always fill a lot of space, nor does a lot of space always require an abundance of fabric, so this distinction

© DAILY MAIL/REX/ALAMY.COM

is important. Volume can be used as a visual symbol of warmth (thick knits, woven woolens, down quilting) or coolness and ventilation (a sundress, caftan, or mumu).

As the human body itself is sculpted naturally by volumes even before it is dressed, designers create shapes to encase, echo, or imitate them, either for function or to tell a story. An abundance of form, horizontal expansion, and increase in fabric and size can emphasize a part of an overall look such as other garments, accessories, or the wearer itself. Adding to the body's original form, volume in fashion construction (continued on page 80)

This strapless, fitted-bodice gown is sculpted by expert seaming techniques to flow from cinched waist to an enormous dome shape, while maintaining a totally smooth surface without collapsing. The crispness of the fabric, its architectural seaming, and the support from the fur beneath it (functional as well as decorative) make this unique form possible.

THIERRY MUGLER,
Paris, France

Carlos Miele

BRAZIL

Carlos Miele is a Brazilian designer who first went global when showing in London, 2002. The son of Italian immigrants who moved to Brazil (he has dual citizenship), he now has boutiques in São Paulo, Rio, Paris, Miami, and New York, while selling in thirty countries. His designs reflect the glamour, color, sensuality, references to nature, and hand-craftsmanship traditions of his native country. He uses crochet, leatherwork, macramé, embroidery, lace, smocking, and other treatments not only to tell his story but also to work with artisan cooperatives in favelas as well as indigenous communities, sustaining Brazilian artisan traditions and recycling materials. There is a philanthropic and social awareness in his production methods and fair-trade practices.

At the same time, he is known for fusing organic forms with high-tech fabrics. His feminine, flowing garments are red-carpet favorites. He also has a lower-priced dress line and a jeans line. He has been showing in New York since 2003 and is a self-taught fashion designer. In 2010, *American Vogue* chose him as the subject for a documentary.

This draped, asymmetrical gown approaches volume another way: Excess fabric is gently controlled in pleated draping that lies flat and fitted across the body, only to be released in billows from the midthigh down to the ankle. Imagine what it feels like to move in this gown! The huge scale of the print is broken up by the diagonal shirring, creating a totally asymmetrical effect. The waterlike flow of the sheer patterned fabric is shattered by the diagonal movements of the pleats, which create their own texture and rhythm. Notice the diagonal neckline draping is exactly opposite the pleating direction in the lower portion. This kind of asymmetry distracts from figure flaws and enhances an organic visual effect that is soothing and sensual.

changes the appearance of the human shape and builds a silhouette. Stiff, light fabrics will radiate outward or upward from the body. (Think ballerina tutu.)

Pleats or gathers and stiffening agents such as horsehair braid, interfacing, boning, and padding are all methods that can hold open space in fabric volume while seam lines, elastic, drawstrings, yokes, and waistbands anchor them to the body through fit or weight. Volume can be found in any location. In a sleeve, it might pop up in a puffed cap, smoothly cut into a deep armhole, gather into a flat or gathered cuff, add width to the elbow level (as in a lantern sleeve), or release

Alaïa blurs the line between garment and accessory in this exploration of the cut-out jacket. An expansive, crisply interfaced nod to the notched collar has width but not height, widening the silhouette in contrast to a double-belted waist and enormous flat-flapped pockets. The structural crocheted bra top follows the contour of the body's anatomy and supports **it. All of this precise and neat detail is relieved by the rows of cowrie-shell fringed volume applied in flirty rows at the hem.**

AZZEDINE ALAÏA,
Paris, France

Sketch, gouache, and pencil. These dresses exemplify how print scale can influence our perception of volume. Still, looks are contrasting with or without the print. The first model has a trapeze top and flared sunburst-pleat skirt with fitted waist, while the second model's silhouette is voluminous through the torso and narrow at shoulders and hem. Both looks are airy, cool, and light.

ADENIYI OKUWOBEJO,
Nigeria/New York, NY, USA

into a wide-open hem. Volume can replace cutting and seaming in loose-fitting batwing, kimono, or dolman sleeves, or between the legs in dropped-crotch pants. Palazzos, bell-bottoms, harem pants, poufed shirts, and jodhpurs all conjure up different locations of bulk. Lengths of fabric can also be secured with pleats or gathers into the waistband or yoke of wide-pegged skirts or trousers with narrow hems. Tiers add fullness one horizontal seam at a time to full skirts or pants.

Volume is recognized immediately in the silhouette of a look. Imagine a skirt with a cinched waist falling into yards of fabric at a voluminous hem! This is achieved with circu-

This gown's superfitted body is offset by the massive sleeves. Microvolume is at work in the yellow hem ruffle, and macrovolume is achieved through the circular flare in the sleeves. The series of exposed African-print darts in the sleeve add rigid bulk to sustain the weight of the fabric in this butterfly silhouette with the help of interfacing.

JEAN PAUL GAULTIER COUTURE,
Paris, France

lar flare (a doughnut-shaped cut of fabric in which the hole becomes the waistline and the outer edges fall in flared ripples) or dirndl construction (a rectangular panel gathered into a waistband or yoke). The slash-and-spread pattern-making technique can be used to add volume to any chosen area in a fitted garment's pattern, whether a straight sleeve, cigarette skirt, collar, or slacks.

With accumulated weight, a fabric's excesses will collapse vertically to the direction of the hem. The location and amount of volume will also affect the function of the form: ease of movement, warmth, flow of fabric, and cost effectiveness. Because excess bulk can make movement difficult, the designer should consider the customer's needs for comfort and mobility.

Remember that volume refers not only to space but also to the sheer quantity of fabric, so it doesn't always denote size. Smocking, shirring, pin tucks, pleats, and origami folds are methods of controlling fabric volume in a flat, secure way, using ample fabric while adhering to a fitted silhouette.

This look's fitted Pucci-esque pant spills upward in golden volume: Fine horizontal pleating visually and structurally supports the blouse's width versus its length. Vertical pleating makes use of the ample fabric in the sleeve, controlled by a fitted, buttoned cuff at three-quarter length. Volume at the shoulder plays off a fitted band-collar neckline echoing the sleeve cuff.

COREY LYNN CALTER,
New York, NY, USA

This series demystifies the concept of the circle skirt. Playing with white and black contrast, the double-faced, clean-finished "doughnut" becomes a skirt. Once anchored on the waist, the fabric weight and thickness falls in clearly defined flares (inverted conical forms of fabric fullness). Armed with needle and thread, the designer takes the circle skirt to another level, anchoring the flares up into a new shape and length.

ALMUDENA ALCAIDE,
New York, NY, USA/Madrid, Spain

Jacqueline Heloise sketches different amounts of volume in relation to a single body. First, a halter top with full-circle and handkerchief hemline; then an A-lined cutaway jacket fitted over a full skirt; and, finally, a semifitted suit that uses horizontal patterning to emphasize its otherwise discreet volume. The emphasis moves from ankle to knee to hip, respectively.

JACQUELINE HELOISE,
New York, NY, USA

func·tion \ fuhngk-shuhn \ *n*
1: the kind of action or activity proper to a person, thing, or institution; the purpose for which something is designed or exists; role. **2:** to have or exercise a function; serve.

10

Function is a marker of garment quality. Every garment aims to serve some set of values among the many ways that fashion can function. At the most basic, humans may adorn themselves for modesty, warmth, or simple decoration. Functions

MOOMOTION/PHOTO: RISHI KUMAR

inspire forms: sleeves, collars, and pants encase cylindrical body forms. Garment components serve as zippers, and buttons open and seal. Patterns decorate, belts secure, and seams join pieces or panels.

Body temperature and climate, freedom of motion, and lifestyle are elemental considerations. Fit is also key. A fitting or fit model session is used to determine that the garment works the way it should, repeatedly, until perfected within delivery time constraints. The sampling/prototyping process perfects a garment until it is as functional as possible before it is offered to the wearer. (continued on page 89)

Quick-drying, color-blocked, poly/lycra knit and stretchy exposed flatlocked seams curve around the body in shapes that cling, ventilate, and reflect for safety.

MOO MOTION,
BY MELISSA MOO,
New York, NY, USA

Stella McCartney

LONDON

Stella McCartney has always designed clothing that she personally would like to wear, making her extremely popular. Her style is confident, clean, constructed, fresh, and feminine.

McCartney graduated in fashion from Central Saint Martins in 1995, and working for Edward Saxon, a Savile Row tailor, was an education in itself.

In 1997, she was appointed creative director of Chloé, successfully revitalizing the brand. McCartney launched her own fashion house, partnering with Gucci in 2001. A conscious vegetarian who lives by the "do unto others as you would have them do unto you," rule, she confidently negotiated an equal partnership, including the stipulation that she would not ever work in fur or leather, and any label that signs with her will have to agree to let her use biodegradable, fake "leathers" and furs. This is a radical commitment for a luxury house and has made her a pioneer in substitute materials.

She expresses surprise at the lack of interest that the fashion industry takes in animal cruelty and environmental concerns and says she prefers to make a small change than do nothing at all. It couldn't be more timely. Designing for a luxury shoe and bag label gives her the opportunity to change the fashion industry from within, and she is doing it beautifully.

At the same time, McCartney doesn't believe that her customer should have to sacrifice anything aesthetic to be environmental or humane. She aims to make the "most exquisitely beautiful, desirable designs possible" consciously, but in such a way that the customer doesn't need to know or notice the difference. Her designs are not recognizably eco in any ostentatious way, nor does she want them to be. This is an interesting distinction. McCartney designs green without pushing the point to sell the clothes. Outside of that quiet yet powerful presence in her brand, she is comfortably outspoken about her beliefs and facts regarding the industry, animal rights, green electricity, food growing, limiting her airplane travel, and conscious impact on the environment. In one interview, she stated clearly that she is not an environmentalist, but a mother (of four), wife, and designer, in that order.

She has an amazingly broad scope of design projects. Aside from her own line is her famous long-term partnership with Adidas, introduced in 2004. The critically acclaimed sports performance collection has since successfully grown to include running, gym, yoga, tennis, swimming, winter sports, and cycling, including the contract to design United Kingdom Olympic uniforms for the Summer Games 2012. In 2011, she designed for the New York City Ballet and presented a one-off capsule evening collection during London Fashion Week. The recipient of international awards too numerous to list here, she funds a new scholarship at Central Saint Martins for designers who adhere to her ethical view. She expresses pride in being able to build her luxury fashion business without using animals, changing the status quo.

Athletic and yogawear inspire this line, and its presentation reiterates the lifestyle and spirit of its customer, from home, to gym, to work, to nightclub, in a playful tone.

BETSEY JOHNSON,
New York, NY, USA

This elegant evening gown's starlike motif decorates the side panel and also creates a minimized silhouette illusion from the front view. The fit is just right.

JULIEN FOURNIE HAUTE COUTURE,
Paris, France

The maillot is fused with a tailored jacket collar in contrasting print to expand swimwear's function and blur definitions.

AGUA BENDITA,
BY CATALINA ALVAREZ
& MARIANA HINESTROZA,
Bogotá, Columbia

A garment may serve a specific category like active sportswear, outerwear, careerwear, lingerie, maternity, eveningwear, costume design, dancewear, bridalwear, or a specific size range such as children, juniors, plus, men, or boys. There are tiers of pricing, production, and distribution methods from mass to couture, as well. All of these call to mind different forms such as fabric quality and construction methods and even colors, level of complexity, conformity, fit, or uniqueness.

A garment speaks, carrying a tone such as sobriety, celebration, formality, playfulness, rebellion, romance, luxury, riotous exuberance, creativity, conformity, or simplicity. In this respect one of its functions is expression. A design may also function to satisfy an approach to design such as economy, minimalism, high performance, rebellion, deconstruction, futurism, or sustainability.

Design choices may be driven by strictly functional needs but usually carry a traditional, historical, or cultural heritage too, incorporating cultural markers such as motifs, colors, raw materials, local crafts and techniques, or silhouettes.

Ample pockets, clingy but stretchy ribbed knits, hoods, adjustable features, buckles and zippers, and waterproof layers might serve the urban nomad in the modern world. Easy care may be a first concern for everyday children's daywear. A nursing mother will have unique, demanding requirements for inner, outer, and undergarments.

Functional clothing solves problems and provides solutions. A piece may be designed to function over or under others, or stand alone. It can be chosen to stand out or to blend into a social setting. While formal occasions might warrant a "made for you" fit and its increased cost, a uniform might put

safety or conformity first. Traveling, nonwrinkling garments are coveted by many today. Functional fabrics may dry fast, absorb, be unisex, or be organic, knit, woven, coated, or stretchy.

Fashion's most basic elements have all evolved out of need. A garment can function to support, mask, imitate, or distort the body's shape; or to enhance, expose, or hide the existing body form. A garment may symbolize membership in a group, subculture, or hierarchy, elevating or masking the social status of the wearer. It may have a readable message or graphic to call out. When a garment functions poorly in one area,

Lingerie goes beyond purely functional and takes on a designer look as a group through coordinated fabrics and details. Pieces are nice enough to be layered and exposed with outergarments and flatter a range of body types with interchangeable silhouettes.

THE LAKE & STARS
COLLECTION
BY MAAYAN ZILBERMAN &
NIKKI DEKKER
New York, NY, USA

Lingerie and swimwear's functions are extended with additional layering pieces and accessories that add to the range of expression for the basic line. Triumph has been designing since 1886, when it began as a southern German corset factory. It is now a major global name with multiple lingerie lines.

usually it is because it was designed for another function. This can also be an inspiration in design.

Global society needs sustainability, a need that fashion is only beginning to learn to serve through zero-waste design, organic and recycled materials, and consciousness of environmental and humane impact of the industry. The textile and garment design and manufacturing systems are going to undergo massive change in this century, as will the consumer's perception of dress, production, and consumption. New business models and technologies will emerge to craft a new era of consciousness that better serves the Earth and its people. Design entails a responsibility that mass production has disconnected over time. The fashion industry is changing its forms in order to serve in this arena, one informed and innovative visionary designer at a time.

Zippers are alienated from their traditional purpose as a closure and playfully used to create an interactive garment with a deconstructed, asymmetrical aesthetic.

ATSURO TAYAMA,
Paris, France

de·con·struc·tion \ ˉde kən 'strək shən \ *n*
1: an approach and aesthetic in which different meanings are discovered by taking apart the structure of a garment's construction method or finish and exposing the assumptions that techniques and components exist only to create a polished exterior appearance.

11

One of the most interesting aspects of late twentieth-century fashion has been the onset of deconstruction, undoing fashion's standards of exclusivity and polished finish and exposing the industry's secrets by putting the formerly hidden,

FIRSTVIEW.COM

unsightly finishes on the outside of the garment and finding the beauty in them—whether
in homage to their careful execution, their
expression of vulnerability and honesty, or to
"deface" hard, glossy, unattainable glamour.

Distressed fabrics, uneven edges, unfinished and unraveling components, or pieces
and parts taken out of their usual context
rethink the purposes and associations linked
to all aspects of garment construction. In
deconstruction, the art and craft of the tailor
is demystified for and exposed to the public,
exposing a world of emotions and possibilities that had been repressed.

(continued on page 96)

**Using only lining fabrics and
notions such as interfacings,
tapes, and belting created to
be hidden in finer garments
creates an exposed fashion
aesthetic that feels fresh and
innovative and educates as
well as fascinates.**

MAISON MARTIN
MARGIELA,
Amsterdam/Paris, France

AFP/GETTY IMAGES

Rei Kawakubo

TOKYO

Rei Kawakubo was born in Tokyo. She is widely recognized as fashion's most forward-pressing innovator and has continuously stretched and pushed fashion structurally, technically, and philosophically in our time, and as an avant-garde artist. Untrained as a fashion designer, she studied fine arts and literature at Keio University in Tokyo. In 1964, she moved into the Harajuku district, where she worked at a textile company before going out on her own as a freelance stylist in 1967.

In 1969, she established Comme des Garçons in Tokyo and opened her first boutique there in 1975. She started designing women's clothes (adding a men's line in 1978), always defying conventional thinking and challenging accepted standards of beauty. Her concepts were so new and shocking, they stirred up strong emotions. She questioned the way women chose clothes, and why, and continues to do so.

Three years later, she started presenting her fashion lines in Paris each season, opening up a boutique in Paris in 1982.

She notes that Western fashion is much slimmer than Japanese fashion, more interested in showing the body's shape. She says that as a Japanese woman, that is not something she is comfortable with. She aims to dress an independent, intelligent woman who doesn't dress to please or seduce others. Her woman is self-sufficient and attracts with a strong mind. During the 1980s, her dark, unusually shaped, seemingly formless garments were the antithesis of the bright, body-conscious fashions of that time.

Kawakubo rejects stereotypes of sexiness and femininity and has stated that the sensuality of clothing comes from the feel of the cloth rather than the way it looks on the body. She likes to give the wearer the freedom to wear the garment in a variety of ways by wrapping. In her mid-'80s collection, Kawakubo created different holes in the garments, allowing the wearer the freedom to put their heads and arms wherever they pleased.

Her silhouettes always invigorate the fashion world with their unique visions, as well as her fabric treatments. Another theme that she innovated was to reverse, invert, and revisit the order of layers in garments, putting vests over jackets, T-shirts over coats, pants belts over blazers, and other unexpected associative and aesthetic ideas. Kawakubo's designs have been described as shapeless, because the shape is not taken from the body's silhouette in the Western sense, but the shapes are very strong and beautiful.

She likes to have input in all the various aspects of her business, rather than just focusing on clothes and accessories. She is greatly involved in graphic design, advertising, and shop interiors, believing that all these things are a part of one vision.

Her design legacy has obviously inspired many avant-garde designers from the 1980s onward, as she provocatively broke open aesthetic, culture, and gender barriers.

Junya Watanabe, Kawakubo's former apprentice, started his own line in the early 1990s and has attained much attention in the fashion business in his own right.

Princess seams, armholes, side seams, and overarm seams are all stitched with the seam allowance to the exterior, decoratively finished with contrast binding—inside-out construction.

AGANOVICH,
BY NANA AGANOVISH
& BROOKE TAYLOR,
London, UK

A long history of corsetry and control in womenswear is still being undone, and advanced, simultaneously by different markets. The tradition of fashion and aristocracy focused on extreme fits, silhouettes, and laborious construction techniques that resulted in clean-finished, "perfect" garments. Construction meant constriction. The aristocracy moved differently than the public, and this was because of their garments.

Deconstruction began with punk and street fashion, slashing and undoing garments for high style and inspiring Vivienne Westwood's and Zandra Rhodes's work. Her deconstruction came from the fact that she,

A historic dress (circa 1851) is reversed for study, revealing a darted pocket bag, hand-finished hems and facings, armhole princess seams, and seam finishes exhibiting fine handwork. Deconstruction takes this to the next level by making exterior beauty from what used to be hidden inside.

COUTURIER CHARLES JAMES,
New York, NY, USA

Classic armhole, neckline, and placket in-one facings and pockets are neatly applied to the outside of the garment in contrast fabric, lending a geometric effect. Ironically, the hem and edges are left raw.

ALEXANDRE HERCHCOVITCH,
São Paulo, Brazil

trained as a textile artist, developed all of her fashion construction techniques on her own. Designers like Sonia Rykiel started to expose seams. Martin Margiela and Rei Kawakubo in the late 1980s and early 1990s revolution-ized fashion as they started to expose its methods and inner structures and train the eye to recognize and find new beauty in the unfinished, torn-apart, reconstructed, and displaced traditions of fashion construction technique. This actually educated the public, revealing fashion's secrets, and unleashed a whole new vocabulary of finishes that are commonly used today.

Exposed boning is applied to the outside of a dress layered over a draped bustline.

KATYA LEONOVICH,
New York, NY, USA

Deconstructing associations and expectations related to fabric use for garments, these looks force new juxta-positions and take fabrics out of their traditional contexts (sweatshirt with fine lace, heavy heathered sweater with evening gown, etc.), and blocking them together into one garment or look.

CANDELA, BY GABRIELA PEREZUTTI,
Uruguay/New York, NY, USA

An exposed, sequined pannier is historical and fantastical. Raw-cut edges, uneven ruffles, exposed tulle underskirts, and a pleated skirt attached to the outside are all manifestations of deconstruction's influence. Young was the creative director at Donna Karan for sixteen years when she launched her children's line and founded Fashion Fights for Children's Rights.

BONNIE YOUNG,
New York, NY, USA

Deconstruction freed (and shocked) the industry, the designer, and the consumer, in contrast to the former dictates of what could and could not be acceptable in dress design. For example, hems no longer had to be carefully folded, interfaced, lined, and in-visibly hand stitched. They might be finished inside out, or even cut and left raw! This previously unthinkable finish has brought previously impossibly light, thin, airy forms into fashion over the past decades.

Deconstruction made fertile ground for creating new forms, doing away with wasteful costs and techniques, opening a space for

humor, unevenness, delicacy, poetry, and a breaking down of social and economic barriers held up by something as seemingly mundane as the way our clothing is made and viewed.

High-low fashion can be considered an aspect of this as well, mixing luxe with bargain basement and restructuring recycled garments. Deconstruction questions everything that is taken for granted in clothing construction, function, and social context.

Fortunately, the implications of deconstruction are social as well as sustainable, as wasteful methods can be cast aside and new methods of creating and re-creating waste can help us reconstruct new models of production and consumption—and style.

A notched, two-piece jacket collar is morphed as the collar portion blends into a hood pattern, creating a new form hybrid with high, wide lapels, and padded jacket shoulders are applied to an evening dress by this jacket-designing duo.

MACKAGE, BY ERAN ELFASSY & ELISA DAHAN, *Montreal, Canada*

neg·a·tive shape \ ˈnegətiv shīap \ *n*
1: a background or ground shape seen in relation to foreground or figure shapes.

12

Negative shape, however subtle, connotes invasion. The fashion garment invades space with its silhouette, cutting into it, or conversely a cutout invades the fashion garment's shape, cutting away from it and exposing skin or layers beneath.

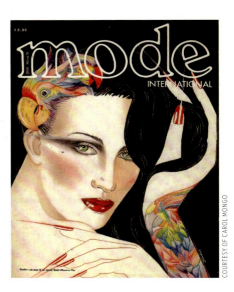

COURTESY OF CAROL MONGO

The edges of that absence create their own shape, referred to as negative shape, or negative space for three-dimensional forms.

Any artist learns to take negative shape into consideration as a lens for viewing things that the untrained eye may not see, providing yet another perspective from which to view, experience, and create design. When viewing negative shapes we temporarily flip our attention to what is not as opposed to what is. The garment silhouette, in this way, can be seen not only as the shape of the garment, but the shape of the garment cuts out of the space surrounding it.

(continued on page 104)

This fashion illustration makes a point of playing the foreground shape off the background to create new shapes and compose the page, intermingling figure, ground, and background with a strong sense of balance.

CAROL MONGO,
Paris, France

The cutout in this garment is totally integrated with the construction, simply resulting from space between bands of gathered silk.

Alix Grès

PARIS

Alix Grès was born Germaine Emile Krebs in Paris, 1903. She always wanted to be a sculptor, "whether in fabric or stone." After studying painting and sculpture, in the 1930s she apprenticed at an Edwardian couture house called Premet for three months, working for the couturier Julie Barton. In the 1930s, during the revival of classicism, her Greek-inspired gowns were born. Her technique of vertical draping was later a great inspiration for Claire McCardell and is recognizably revisited time and time again by prominent designers decade after decade. This was her favorite theme, which she continued to work over her career, always varied with daring cutouts and new interpretations. Each 7-centimeter band of gathered silk was condensed out of 2.5 meters!

Technically, she is also greatly known for her use of dolman sleeves and bias cuts. In the 1950s and 1960s, her designs became more focused on tailoring and suits. Grès's work runs the gamut from finely controlled, delicate, draped column dresses to carefully sculpted, clean-shaped silhouettes. Her strong-shaped garments used the weight and character of the fabric itself to create integrated structure instead of using crinolines or other structural supports, and most styles were unembellished and monochromatic. The garments were designed to be worn without support. While she individually draped each one in the round, sketching was also part of her process, evidenced by Pierre Bergé's collection of her sketches. Apparently simple line drawings, they make visual notes of her ideas in an abstract, quick form.

Her colors remain constant over her six-decade career—rust red, green, daffodil yellow, chestnut—with a natural feel, which all appeared on a single dress in the 1970s. She was elected president of the Chambre Syndicale de la Haute Couture in the 1970s and awarded their highest honor, the De D'Or (Gold Thimble).

When Grès's company dissolved, Azzedine Alaïa collected her pieces for the Marseille fashion museum. A 2011 exhibit of her work at the Musée Bordelle in Paris featured her pieces among sculptures, in honor of her initial dream.

Negative space formed by the asymmetrical neckline shaping is sensual and relaxed. At right, a knitted dimensional form creates a rhythm down a sleeve edge. A semisheer insert shape almost separates the sleeve from the shoulder seam at right, and slashes and holes become part of the surface play of the knit.

GUY LAROCHE,
Paris, France

COURTESY OF CHERYL KOO, CREATOR OF THE OTHER DUCK, USA

From the profile, a play of surfaces and deconstruction cut into the background and edges expose skin. A ribbed waistband hugs behind, while a tailored front with shirttail shaping extends the front hemline dramatically. This extension is balanced by a voluminous hood at the top of the silhouette.

CHERYL KOO, CREATOR OF THE OTHER DUCK,
Los Angeles, CA, USA

This illustration in gouache captures only the negative shape (the skin), leaving the clothing, hairstyle, and shoes to the imagination.

LAURA VOLPINTESTA,
New York, NY, USA

A basic vocabulary of negative shapes cut into garments to form the basic foundations of standard fashion forms: the neckline cutout, V-neck, or scoop back. Moving down along the silhouette, there may be bustline or midriff cutouts, a bare back, cinched waist, notched collar edges carved out in various shapes, or scalloped edges. Visible or not, the space between the garment and the wearer creates a negative shape as well, that is felt, even if not seen. This can be considered in terms of fit, or discussed in terms of ease (the amount of wiggle room built into a garment), or may refer to an abundant space that moves independently of the body.

The spaces between garments in a lineup of models create shapes by absence, creating shapes between shapes. In layouts of sketches or illustrations, the spaces and shapes between models are considered in the design of the overall page for a dynamic and deliberate composition. Every element added to a presentation has impact on the space surrounding it through both its obvious positive shape character and the negative shapes it carves out of its surroundings.

A negative shape can punctuate the space around it with a rhythm or a pattern of forms, such as a silhouette edged with layers,

Midriff cutouts and double ties, along with the single shoulder, cut into the shape of the standard maillot (and create interesting tan lines).

CIA MARITIMA,
BY PATRIZIA SIMONELLI
& MARCELLA SANT'ANNA,
Rio de Janeiro, Brazil

A stretch pantsuit uses seaming and panels to play with the direction of stripes and enhance the body shape. The drawstring halter bodice interlaces with cutouts at center front and side waist, the negative shapes interacting with a layered jacket and scarf.

FUTURE CLASSICS,
BY JULIE WILKINS,
London, UK

Layers, uneven hemlines, and contrasting tones play up the interaction of shapes over the figure and between garments for a dynamic effect.

ANNE BOWEN,
New York, NY, USA

Contrast trim on edges, cuffs, and cutouts with exposed skin characterize the work of this designer, emphasizing the ways in which garment edges carve into the body, background, and garment, creating strong negative shapes. The fringe creates a softer negative shape.

KATYA LEONOVICH,
New York, NY, USA

tiers, quilted puffs, fur, or knitted bumps. It might cut out the form of a hood (rounded or pointed, slouchy or rigid), a sleeve, or a massive skirt. It can cut into space decidedly with an opaque, rigid form, or perhaps shyly with a perforated, broken, or sheer veil of a shape. Considering both positive and negative shape in design heightens awareness, expands vocabulary, and offers more to work with in creating and manipulating form in space.

Arzuaga always focuses on clean shapes. This puff shoulder punctuates the background space with its volume, as does the wide skirt form. Sheer fabric suspended into space makes a point of exposing the negative space between garment and body.

AMAYA ARZUAGA,
Madrid, Spain

sym·me·try \ sim-i-tree \ *n*
1: the correspondence in size, form, and arrangement of parts on opposite sides of a plane, line, or point; regularity of form or arrangement in terms of like, reciprocal, or corresponding parts. **2:** the proper or due proportion of the parts of a body or whole to one another with regard to size and form; excellence of proportion. **3:** beauty based on or characterized by such excellence of proportion.

13

Symmetry is balance. The scale tips neither one way nor the other. Bilateral reflection of the left repeats on the right in symmetry. The center front line, from the part of the hair, nose, center of chin, heart center, navel, between the ankles, divides

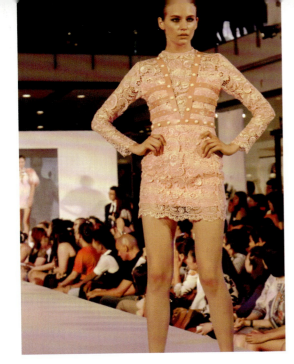

Perfectly symmetrical and even, paired with crisply constructed solid pieces of graphic patterning and natural-toned organic textile fibers and weaves, come to the fore in careful proportions of shape and texture.

the body into halves. The center front line on a fashion pattern piece can be place on a folded piece of fabric, traced, cut, and opened to create a basic garment. Collars, pockets, front, and back zippers love reflections. Symmetry points to the center of the look, and this irresistible focus is soothing, grounding, centering.

There is something in us that craves balance and predictibility at times. Symmetry need not mean boring or square; actually, it opens up room for a lot of other improvisations. When a garment is draped on the form, or designed through flat pattern, often (continued on page 112)

Textures and surfaces in monochromatic tints are strictly symmetrical and structured, yet lighthearted and feminine in detail, color, trims, and fabric choices.

PRANG FOR ACCADEMIA ITALIANA,
Bangkok, Thailand

Sergio Davila

PERU

A native of Peru, and, grandchild of European immigrants, Sergio Davila graduated from the Academy of Art University in San Francisco in 2002 and immediately began developing and creating his own menswear line based on a vision for how he wanted to dress. He started as the tailor, designer, and businessman. His first collection immediately generated interest on the West Coast, finding immediate buyers with established retailers. The Hispanic Scholarship Foundation chose to include the collection in a charity fashion show in San Francisco.

In February 2004, Davila's fall/winter collection was launched to critical acclaim, and in March 2004, the first Sergio Davila Menswear store opened in Manhattan. In spring/summer 2008, the collection was shown at the Chelsea Art Museum during New York Fashion Week.

Sergio Davila was the winner of Fashion Group International's Rising Star Award for Best Menswear Designer 2009 in New York, finally showing at Bryant Park.

At the beginning of 2010, he was one of the nominees for Best Menswear Designer of the Ecco Domani Fashion Foundation. In mid-2010, Collezioni magazine selected his spring/summer 2010 collection as one of the most representative menswear collections at New York Fashion Week.

His design offers balance, creating a look of sportswear sophistication doused with strong touches of warmth, using ultrasoft fabrics including pima cottons and alpaca blend with silk, all 100 percent organic. Knits and geometric woven patterns abound in his work. The geometric shapes of his garments often mimic the woven forms in his patterns.

During Mercedes Benz Fashion Week in New York (spring/summer 2009), Davila featured his creations inspired by the 1930s emigration of Europeans into Peru (like his grandparents). The design is comfortable, casual, elegant, and easy to dress up or down. Some of the pieces are very interseasonal in concept by simply adding or subtracting layers, and consequently very practical.

Davila has collaborated with Loredana Cannia, a master of twisting threads for outstanding knitwear, creating one-of-a-kind pieces of art. All of his collections emphasize the quality of natural, 100% organic, textiles, an intelligent style conceived in the United States with influence from techniques used in Peruvian knitwear, woven patterns, and textiles as well as Lima's rich culture.

only half is draped. There is a consciousness in every choice along the way that the half-design will be reflected when executed in the whole. Still, there is a sense of surprise when the first test is cut out of the whole garment and the full effect is observed.

The human body and skeleton are basically symmetrical from the front and back view. Fashion sketches often focus on these views, which are wider and have the full impact of the look, but wouldn't it be interesting to begin the design process from the side seam instead of center front or back? The center front is the most dominant feature of a look and always has this capacity to be

The illustration is symmetrical at first glance, revealing unique details in the jacket designs. The symmetry creates a beautiful negative shape between the two models.

ELEONORA GENDLER,
Brooklyn, NY, USA

Totally symmetric, edgy, textural, and cutaway silhouettes mingle large, clean shapes with intricate detailing that requires careful construction. Even the hairstyle is split evenly on the center front line.

MARIA KE FISHERMAN,
Madrid, Spain

Futuristic while inspired by nature, these microforms built into macro shapes are strictly symmetrical, yet are gorgeously designed from every angle in sculptural form.

EVA SOTO CONDE,
Madrid, Spain

Classic elegance and clean-cut construction are perfectly refined and balanced in yarn-dyed plaids laying out evenly over the center line, with alternating contrast grain direction on placket, cuffs, collar and pocket flaps, for movement and interest.

SLAVA ZAITSEV
COLLECTION,
Moscow, Russia

reflective along the center line. Symmetry need not be all or nothing. A symmetrical bodice may have an uneven hemline, or a symmetrical outfit may feature an unbalanced surface pattern texture or that blurs the reflection of the shape.

Anything as basic as a tailored jacket, though perhaps designed around a symmetrical vision, is inherently asymmetric when the front overlaps for closure, however subtle this may be. Jeans open on center front, but the fly structure, button, and stitching are actually sightly off to one side. A vent in the center back of a coat may direct all of the facing excess to one side, creating a knife pleat, of sorts.

Something about symmetry is ideal, striving for perfection, and feels controllable in a sometimes-chaotic world. Symmetry's prevalence in fashion is related to its processes such as pattern making and draping; its raw material, which is often folded and cut; and its best friend, the human body, which is symmetrical in nature. It might be said that symmetrical garments are "primary," as asymmetry seems to be a variation on this primordial form.

It is interesting that the existence of a definitive center in symmetry emphasizes a sense of radiating forms from that center, which always point back to the core of the human body. This radiant aspect can have a spiritual nature that focuses on the heart of the individual, no matter what their clothes are saying otherwise.

Body-clinging minidresses emphasize the symmetry of an hourglass silhouette, with cinched waist, lightly padded shoulders, color-blocked style lines, sheer cutouts, and flirtatious embellishments following its balanced form. Each seam follows the body's shape to make a fitted piece.

ELFS, BY TANDARIĆ IVAN & ALEKSANDER SEKULIJICA
Zagreb, Croatia

a·sym·me·try \ ey-sim-i-tree \ *n*
1: lack of balance or symmetry

14

asymmetry

Fabric, whether knitted or woven, is a symmetrical raw material, rectangularly produced in bands by hand or machine. A minimally cut square woven or knitted piece of fabric, joined at the shoulders or side seams, creates simple, clean, symmetric

shapes, like the poncho, caftan, gathered-waist skirt (dirndl), or drop-crotched pant by cutting half shapes on a fold of fabric and opening them into a bilaterally symmetrical form. Most likely, saris, scarves, and wrapped pieces of woven cloth tied onto the body introduced the first ventures into asymmetry in dress as fabric was pulled or draped across and around the figure. Overlapping front-edge closures, surplice fronts, wrap skirts, double-breasted jackets and coats, or symmetrical garments cut from different colors or textures for each side, are moderate design ventures into asymmetry.

(continued on page 120)

Color blocking and piecing along seam lines is surprising in this armhole-princess line fitted sheath, catching the eye immediately with its thoughtful improvisation to a piece that might otherwise be harshly square.

ATELIER SWAROVSKI,
BY PRABAL GURUNG,
Singapore/New York, NY, USA

Uneven necklines and hemlines with cut-out effects and straps counteract swirling original patterns with clean borders, carving beautiful shapes out of the arms, neckline, and legs. Irregularity is the norm.

Katya Leonovich

NEW YORK

Katya Leonovich is a Moscow-born designer based in Manhattan since 2009. She graduated from the Academy of Fine Arts in Moscow, studying fine arts, then fashion, and uses her trained art eye for her design, as well as her paintings for fabric designs. She also lived and worked in France and Italy at the house of Gattinoni, which focused on embroideries, corsets, and luxury dresses and made her aware that she wanted to create a new vision of fashion. Considering Rome her second home, she is inspired by the many differences in each city's architecture, the colors, the different types of people, their styles of dressing, and the musicality of their languages. All of these aspects inform her artistic vision. Her abstract vision liberates her from traditional dressmaking's perspective.

One of her fashion shows was an installation that featured her large, colorful paintings as the backdrop for her fashion models, and you could see the direct correlation of her magical color sense and aesthetic. In her spring/summer 2011 runway show, she began to paint live onto a couture bridal gown during the show.

Starting her career by entering competitions, she has won the Mittelmodal Prize, the Smirnoff International Competition, the Nadejda Lamanova Prize of the Russian Federation, and Supima's inaugural Competition for Emerging Designers. L Gallery in New York had a retrospective exhibit of her designs. She represents the new generation of Russian fashion, according to *Russia's Encyclopedia of Fashion*.

Her "Beautiful Garbage" design aesthetic, couture techniques, and bold-painted digital prints are unique and definitive of her style. Based on the idea that beauty doesn't last forever, driving her to constant creation, it embraces the freedom to find beauty in what has been cast aside, like discarded scraps of fabric.

Her collections balance solid neutrals in firm fabrics with soft, wild, colorful, dreamy prints on soft, shiny, or thin fabrics such as fur, wool, silk, leather, gauze, and chiffon. Asymmetry, cutouts, and leather are also outstanding features in her work along with corsetry and draping. Soft and hard also always find a balance in her collections.

Leonovich's design concept revolves around her belief in "Beautiful Garbage." She incorporates fabrics of chiffon and silks with unexpected materials including torn paper, pieces of aluminum, feathers, and fringes. A pair of her dresses made to walk the runway together featured paintings of Mitt Romney and Barack Obama. She has a lighthearted joy and love of art and life that infuses her work and personality. Not a trend follower, she aims to use modern silhouettes but infuse new and futuristic ideas while still keeping it wearable.

Her inspirations are more abstract, never about a singular theme or idea. To keep it relevant, she designed a recent collection for the women in her New York neighborhood, based on what she wished they would wear. She also designs for men, but with less color and more minimal style.

There is nowhere for the eye to rest following edges in this look that plays on tones of a single color cut in diagonal lines all around the body. The tonal fabric play emphasizes seam angles.

NARCISO RODRIGUEZ,
New York, NY, USA

A symmetrical garment with a motif or embroidery on one side, or a single pocket on a jacket or shirt breast, are examples of gently uneven detailing that shift the visual balance of a garment, adding interest.

Single-shouldered bodices, single sleeves, and uneven hemlines on sleeves or skirts have more pronounced asymmetry. Garments that are fitted on only one side, or short on one side, or that have seemingly random drapes or seams running diagonally from one side of the body to the other, suddenly make the effect more overt and deliberate.

Asymmetry plays up organic form, seeming to diminish the controlled, sometimes mechanical approach of Western fashion, especially in mass production. In asymmetry, lines seem to spiral and wind around the body, making it difficult for the eye to rest in any one place. This distracts from the unevenness of our own bodies' details, which are assumed to be totally symmetrical yet are full of gentle nuances that reflect our own inexact nature.

Breaking the predictability of symmetry interacts with the observer as it brings visual expectations into question, drawing the eye

Monochromatic looks and the play of draping reveal off-centered design as the focus of this collection. There is a confidence and mastery of technique in the development of these garments.

ALLDRESSEDUP, BY LIONEL LEO & TINA TAN LEO
Kuala Lumpar, Malaysia

from left to right, top to bottom, following details sequentially and provoking curiosity about the process that led the designer to their decisions.

While often reflecting a mastery of craft that a designer uses to innovate fashion's forms in the avant-garde, asymmetry can also communicate a return to origins, as pure as the first time a length of woven or knitted fabric was tossed over a shoulder, wrapped, or tied onto the human form. In this way, asymmetry can express a purity, a return to the preindustrial, improvised forms of dress in which the wearer created the garment's shape on her body for a custom fit.

Saufi drapes her specialty, local traditional ikats and batiks, across the hips or shoulders for dynamic flow, always playing off a symmetrical base with no zips or buttons.

TOM ABANG SAUFI,
Kuala Lumpar, Malaysia

Cutouts, transparency, exposed seams, lines, texture blocking, and draping take a turtlenecked minidress silhouette into asymmetrical variations of texture and pattern.

AGANOVICH, BY NANA AGANOVICH & BROOKE TAYLOR,
London, UK

In tropical regions, warmth coverage is no concern, and so single sleeves, cutouts, and off-shoulder necklines are more prevalent, as is wrapped-on fashion. Off-balanced fashion need not be synonymous with unresolved. To the contrary, often it provides the visual softness that we crave as humans, but it can take quite a bit of work for a designer to accomplish technically in tailored garments.

A symmetrical dress silhouette is broken up by asymmetrical detailing including seaming, piecing, fabric blocking, and surface detail: neckline appliqué and diagonal rows of ruffle across the dress shape resulting in a complex design.

ANA BALBOA,
London, UK/Madrid, Spain

Sheer, opaque, black, white, and reflective all come together with a strong sense of balance in this asymmetrical look.

DEMI PARKCHOONMOO,
Seoul, South Korea

trans·par·en·cy \ tran'spar∂nse \ *n*
1: the quality of being able to be seen through. Transparency exposes, reveals, and creates ghostlike shells with shapes beneath. Our skin's opacity hides what is inside us, and garments can hide our skin, but transparent layers and garments can offer a peek at whatever the designer chooses. Using transparency, a large, loose garment can still show the definition of the body inside or garment layers beneath.

15

Sheer fabrics usually create a smoke-screen effect. Woven and finely knit sheers are never totally sheer like a vinyl could be, and yet vinyl is reflective. The cloudy, hazy effect of a sheer fabric softens any look, color, or surface. Coincidentally,

such fabrics are often soft to the touch, though not necessarily so.

Sheer fabrics reveal their construction: French seams, labels, plackets, pleats, stitching—all of it becomes visible to the eye as an opaque brushstroke on the sheer canvas. Sheer is sensual in its generosity; as many garments are seen as highly protective shells, sheer fabrics invite and offer up vulnerability.

Often existing in degrees and gauges of visibility, from cotton lawn, batiste, organza, chiffon, and tulle, to the openwork of bobbin lace, fishnet, mesh, eyelet or filet crochet, to slashed denim or perforated leather, sheer (continued on page 130)

It seems that the umbrella inspired the jacket. Perfect for exposing a tailored suit beneath, a clean-lined, clear vinyl trench edged in white binding exposes every border and seam intentionally, including pocket bags and side seams, creating an x-ray vision of the jacket structure and showing off its carefully planned lines. Here, shiny vinyl transparency reflects the light that a rainy day needs and resembles the water it repels. A-lined hem, capelike collar, and umbrella all extend from a tied-front waist.

ROBERTO VERINO,
Madrid, Spain

Zandra Rhodes

LONDON

Zandra Rhodes (born 1940, England), is the daughter of a fashion fitter and lecturer at Medway College. She studied printed textile design at the Royal College of Art in London, graduating in 1964. She developed her own techniques for cutting (minimally to preserve the integrity of the textile design), constructing, and finishing her garments, made from her own prints (usually on sheer silk chiffons). Her patterns and styles are bold, but her medium so sheer and soft that the clothes become feminine and gentle.

In 1984, the book *The Art of Zandra Rhodes,* which was rereleased in 1995, exposed the process behind her fabric designs and themes behind each collection. It is amazing to see how her garments look and move on a model and how her highly evolved textiles exist as stand-alone art (often drawn with linear elements and "squiggles" around a theme, and including borders and placed patterns in favor of typical allover industrial print repeats). The textile is usually created first and is highly valued, much like in ethnic dress, so her garments are not usually excessively cut or pieced, though the construction details are meticulously hand finished.

Her work merits viewing "flat on the table" as well as on a model to understand the form, philosophy, proportions, and aesthetic. Laid flat, her book refers to her pieces as "butterflies," with their winged sleeves; slashed, finished fringes; and handkerchiefed hems that resemble their namesake.

She always remained true to her own methods and aesthetics and had an intense work ethic, known for hand rolling the yards of fine silk hems in her creations and innovating the way that print screens could be created to serve the use of the print on the garment. Carefully archiving her work throughout her career, Rhodes developed each season with deep personal relevance and craft, operating in a way that is very rare for a designer today. She maintained samples of every piece she ever made and catalogued the history of her work.

Rhodes always had unique haircuts and colors and used nontraditional makeup colors to create her own personal look that transcended to her designs. One of her collections was a slashed jersey group in 1977, joined with safety pins that linked her later to the punk style. Some clients include Jerry Hall, Freddie Mercury, Elizabeth Taylor, Bianca Jagger, and Joan Rivers. Her vintage clothes are sought by fashionistas and top designers today, worn by icons such as Naomi Campbell and Kate Moss, and Sarah Jessica Parker on *Sex and the City.* Most major fashion museum collections in the world have her pieces, and she has garnered numerous awards and been featured on a British postage stamp. In 2001, she started designing opera sets in the United Kingdom and abroad.

Rhodes set up the Fashion and Textile Museum in London in 2003, which features designers from 1950s onward. In 2006, she designed a makeup capsule collection for MAC cosmetics and clothing lines for Marks and Spencer and Topshop. She has had solo exhibits almost every year since 1978 and various retrospectives.

Zandra Rhodes is notorious for designing her own prints on fine silk chiffon and meticulously finishing, hand rolling, or beading the often-zigzagged or fringed edges. This 2007 look carries on her tradition in a sheer caftan exemplifying her self-taught, folkloric shapes that have followed her and evolved from the beginning, and also reveals the complexity of her patterns (even in a two-color print). The variety of patterns within a single panel are hand-drawn linear motifs, with the planned placement hitting the body in certain areas.

FIRSTVIEW.COM

Classic combinations of fabric blocking and fresh, trend-proof silhouettes cross cultures. Layering a long tunic shirtdress over stovepipe trousers would get heavy if not for the clever printed chiffon panels that make up the length of it. The engineered print runs from floral to solid black with dots without a seam, perfectly centered on the piece.

DURO OLOWU,
Lagos, Nigeria/London, UK

A totally transparent, highly reflective, and playful showstopper is built from permanent, seamed bubbles of varying scales, creating a wide silhouette and rhythmic pattern of round edges over a flat, linear-banded, opaque, cut-out maillot base. Cutouts are another aspect of magnified transparency.

NINA RICCI,
Paris, France

A sheer layer of matte green chiffon over a white charmeuse base reveals a hazy impression of a tuxedo-front shirt's formality, without any of the bulk, printed on the underlayer. This shirt is created with a single, center back seam (eliminating the side seam), and unconventional exposed darts at the shoulder reveal the contrast lining.

LES FILLES, BY EDWIN AKABA & CAROLINE ROSSIGNOL,
New York, NY, USA

can always play out in a new and surprising way. Transparency enjoys its many manifestations, and layering sheer over sheer often creates a level of opacity.

What is it about sheer that is so dreamy? Possibly the remembrance that forms may not be as solid as they appear, that one could put one's hand through a solid form, like a cloud, a fence, or a pool of water. Transparency can shock, reveal, gently hide, interact, gently protect, line, fade, or confuse our ideas about what is solid and what is not.

Sheer garments reveal their insides to the outside and even expose their construction, which, as we know, takes a lot of confidence and builds intimacy. Transparency is emotionally, then, related to trust.

It's hard not to notice that the weighty updo on the model is so much more dense, though similar in shape, than the sheer, frothy, wiry, irregular forms at the hem of this unique silhouette. Sculptural, exploratory, gravity-defying, weblike fabric extends beyond an opaque column in tiers, using varying degrees of circular flare and a rigid hem. The fabrics are sheer, but varying in textures and patterns.

CELIA KRITHARIOTI,
Athens, Greece

Opaque throughout the torso, a floor-length, full-skirted silhouette is deconstructed, exposing a tulle crinoline with wide, bias-taped finish to create weight and form with rolling, rounded flares spiraling from hip to floor. The sheer skirt visually lightens what would be a heavy, formal look and keeps the body in view where there is volume. The visible, structural hem finish becomes decorative.

VICTOR DE SOUZA,
*Buenos Aires, Argentina/
New York, NY, USA*

Here, sheer black reveals shiny, baby-pink sequins beneath. Opaque fine piping at the neckline pairs with spaghetti straps, opaque shiny bands hem bell sleeves, overlapping sheers create an opaque center to the look, with diagonal seaming creating lines across the body.

KLÛK CGDT,
BY MALCOLM KLÛK
& CHRISTIAN GABRIEL
DU TOIT,
Cape Town, South Africa

Sheer organza alternates with opaque embellishment as an allover pattern applied by hand over the bust area without becoming too heavy. Intended, or not, the skin tone becomes a ground color in the blouse, while the pouf skirt, stuffed with gathered tulle, is grounded in cream. The effect is feminine, delicate, handcrafted, and plays with the idea of one garment or two. The two pieces are one, and yet it is divided by the opacity, and the condensed patterning of the skirt versus the spread-out top.

TERESA HELBIG,
Madrid, Spain

lay·er \ ley-er \ *n*
1: a thickness of some material laid on or spread over a surface. **2:** one of several items of clothing worn one on top of the other.

16

A textile that forms the basis for every garment
is essentially planar—wide, relatively flat, and has
a face. This face becomes an edge when seen in
profile, or when its boundaries are cut, finished,
or formed. Once these edges begin to multiply

into cuts sitting on top of one another, as by layering garments, or by adding layered forms such as pocket flaps, collars, or decorative pieces to a garment, the depth of space is emphasized. What is on the surface interacts with what lies beneath, casting shadows, emphasizing differences in weight or surface, and extending form from the core of the body outward, into the outside world.

In early Western fashion, cotton or silk undergarments, white, natural, and washable, always provided a hygienic layer of comfort, absorbency, and cushion between the wearer and the main garment, even when comfort (continued on page 136)

Eveningwear, with ultrafine layers of organza and angled corners that craft decorative effects through layering, looks delicate and sharp at the same time, executed with extreme care.

ANGEL SANCHEZ,
Caracas, Venezuela/
New York, NY, USA

Born in 1938 in Hiroshima, Japan, Issey Miyake says he was first made aware of the link between design and emotion by Isamu Noguchi's bridges, "To Live" and "To Die" (now renamed "To Create" and "To Go"). Walking and watching these bridges, he realized the power in the experience of inspired design.

In 1960, the World Design Conference was held in Japan, and Miyake wrote a letter asking why clothing design was not included. After he graduated with a degree in graphic design, he designed his first collection: "poems of cloth and stone."

In 1965, he went to Paris and studied haute couture, then worked as an assistant for a fashion designer. Away from home, living and working in Paris, Miyake asked himself what he could say in fashion. He realized that freedom from Western tradition or convention was his advantage. Anything he would do in Western tradition would be new for him, and his heritage would be a novelty in Paris—a perfect setting for exploring contemporary and universal fashion, beyond cultural boundaries. Miyake is always recognized for blurring the line between art and clothing/fashion, and East and West. His work brings new realities to life, creating forms and materials for the human body that have never been seen before. Respecting the kimono's relationship to the body, he believes that clothes should fit, but easily, not constricting, creating bold shape, and using natural closures such as ties.

Miyake's work is highly collaborative and focuses on fusing new textiles and forms with the latest technologies, previously unexplored materials, and reviving traditional dyeing and weaving techniques, bringing them back to life in new ways for a

Issey Miyake

TOKYO

contemporary lifestyle. His collaborations with manufacturers, artisans, new digital technology, and artists realize new possibilities in textile patterns and textures.

In 1978, *Issey Miyake: East Meets West* was published, including photos by Irving Penn and essays by artists about his work. In the 1980s, he started Plantation, a clothing line that addressed people's everyday needs by using primarily natural materials and a focus on handcrafts in comfortable, loose designs. In 1985, he launched Miyake Permanente, a line based on previously launched designs intended to be long-lasting, classic pieces. In the early 1990s,

Pleats Please was launched. Knitted and sewn first, the garments were permanently pleated in a heat press. It was his unique way to create modern, durable, universal, and beautiful clothes for modern life.

His A-Poc (A Piece of Cloth) collaboration with Dai Fujiwara (who became the creative director of Issey Miyake in 2006) created seamless, tubular garments from a single thread, with suggestive lines embedded in them that the consumer could use as a guideline for customizing the garment by cutting to different lengths, sleeves, and necklines. Custom-made clothing, without sweat shops, without hours of labor. It

was innovative, creative, and sustainable fashion in which the consumer collaborates with the designer.

Since 2004, the Issey Miyake Foundation trains professionals and introduces young artists from all over the world. In 2007, his 21_21 Design Sight center published literature and organized exhibitions and events in Tokyo. Currently, his Reality Lab design team deals with design and society, including the development of environmentally friendly (recycled PET polyester, for example) and resource-conscious materials to make and re-create new designs and techniques.

was not a first priority. The layers of corsetry, panniers, crinolines, and the like supported garments and functioned to hold their fitted shape. Bloomers, blouses, and petticoats contributed to a silhouette as undergarments that peeked out at edges, adding to the overall look.

The Japanese tradition of layering looser garments has become more prevalent in the fashion landscape over the past half century. This kind of dressing takes emphasis away from clinging to the body's form.

Layering garments opens up the field for play in proportion, as each garment layer has its own proportional story of length,

Soft tones of fluttering silk with fine edges and varying surfaces and weights are layered into long, lightweight, narrow silhouettes.

FABIO COSTA,
BELO HORIZONTE,
Minas, Brazil

Layers are mixed with blocked textures within individual garments for a totally broken-up look. Kokosolaki's line intentionally encourages the wearer to engage in the improvisation by piling on choice garments to make a silhouette and texture story.

DIESEL BLACK GOLD, BY SOPHIA KOKOSOLAKI, *Athens, Greece/London, UK*

width, and texture within it. Juxtapose this with the garment beneath it, the human beneath that, and the garment over or underneath that, and you may have chaos or order, but you will always have a story.

Fashion has its conventions of layering garments. This was taken for granted before deconstructionists, most notably Rei Kawakubo, started reversing the order by layering belts over jackets, shrunken tees over bulky knits, vests over coats. Breaking this restriction opened up design to a new range of fresh and surprising looks. Proportions and layers have an exchange when shirt hems peek out from beneath jacket hems, while

Layered original patterns in knit create warmth while piling voluminous pieces over a clingy foundation.

STEPHANIE GELOT, *Ontario, Canada*

Strong tonal classics are layered in subtly, unusually proportioned menswear-inspired separates, close to the body.

CHERYL CHEE,
Australia/Tokyo, Japan

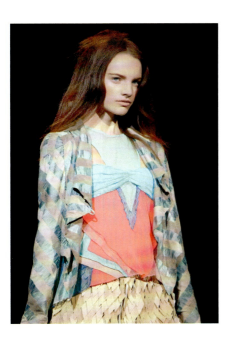

Visually intersecting lines and planes, through fabric blocking and optical layering, create the illusion of layers in space. Tiny overlapping shapes create an overall textural pattern on the skirt with repeating form, and, of course, the garments are layered, too.

CUSTO BARCELONA,
BY CUSTO DALMAU,
Barcelona, Spain

layering over skirts and trousers layered over stockings and boots, at every possible length and width along the human form, symmetrically or asymmetrically, a textural, proportional, and visual effect is created. Layering increases the options for mixing "high-low" fashion as garments from different designers and price points are pulled together for a unique look authored by the wearer. Silhouettes can be built out of mixed shapes. Finally, layering frees the wearer to adjust their look according to the needs of their lifestyle, by removing and adding pieces at a moment's notice.

In garment construction, layers of interfacing, linings, and structural layers contribute to garment weight, behavior, and performance. Layering features such as peplums, collars, appliqués, tiers, pocket flaps, or folds of decorative fabric onto or into the garment shell are expressions of beauty or necessity, with proportions chosen by the wearer or the aesthetics of the designer.

A recurring theme of superimposition is rich and decorative, whether heavy woolens or delicate lace; each subsequent layer peeks through visibly, carrying the eye through depth of space and preciously surrounding the wearer.

CHRIS BENZ,
New York, NY, USA

tex·ture \ teks-cher \ *n*
1: the visual and, especially, tactile quality of a surface.

17

Whether played up or down, texture is always present, as textile naturally lends texture. Designers discussing fabric selections for a piece or group don't just look at swatches, they touch,pinch, bend, feel, wrap, squeeze, and fold them with their fingers

A macrotexture is created by exposed stretchy 1/8-inch overlock seams webbing over the body. Opposite at right, a seafoam green suede halter explores both sides of the skin, for smooth and rough surface contrast as well as tonal play.

to compute their quantitative and qualitative combination of characteristics: rigidity or fluidity, weight, gauge, thickness, "give" or stretchability, matte, gloss, or satiny finish.

Whether in mohair, terry cloth, burlap, cheesecloth, gauze, crinkle, washed silk, lambskin, China silk, seersucker, crepe-backed satin, tweed, chenille, hand knit, tulle, matte jersey, cavalry twill, vinyl, or stone-washed denim, texture behaves undeniably, be it surface, thickness or thinness, bumps, scratchy grains, slubby yarns, or flocking.

At first glance, pattern and color can move texture down the sensory priority list, (continued on page 144)

Head to toe texture in Tokyo. From teased hair, flowing ribbons, and fabric flowers to lace gloves, circular cut-out hose, tiers of tulle, and an exposed crinoline, the look is executed in crème and paper white, bringing to fore textural aspects, exposing the play of shadow over and under the stiff fabric's cuts, layers, pleats, and gathers. Note the texture's behavior across the surface as well as throughout the edge and contours of this silhouette.

TOKYO STREET PHOTOGRAPHY, UNKNOWN DESIGNER

Lily Blue

LONDON/LOS ANGELES

Lily Blue, named after a princess and her cat, was born in London in 1982. Brought up in a bohemian household by her mother, Mariora Goschen, a potter and acupuncturist, and her grandmother, Angela, a sculptress, painter, and seamstress, art was in her blood from the very beginning. She describes the moment when she woke from a lucid dream with the undeniable urge to design clothes. "From that day on, I would take apart my thrift shop clothes to understand how they were made. That is how I taught myself." Today, she is a creative artist, designer, and photographer.

After studying dance and theater in London, Blue began a period of extensive travel, which influenced her unique take on life and can be found in every stitch of her designs. She worked in a South African dance troupe, where she explored the shape of bodies in motion, and a diving center in Egypt, with underwater coral landscapes that inspired her use of colors and textures. Her work in improvisational theater, in London and Los Angeles, also influenced her dramatic and sometimes edgy silhouettes.

Upon return from her travels, Blue took an internship at Vivienne Westwood, where she had the great fortune to work close to the "Queen of Couture" herself. Blue studied the way Westwood had mastered her craft, continuously broke conventions, and was inspired by the genius she observed.

Soon after this, she moved to California, opening her first studio. Interest in her clothes began to spread, and the Lily Blue label was born.

Blue encourages women to see their inner beauty and embrace their bodies, souls, and potential. "The fashion industry tends to have an unhealthy approach to the body. I want all my models to be strong and not adhere to this awful sense of perceived beauty, which is so prevalent and idolized in the media. My clothing is about accentuating the feminine spirit as well as her form—not catering to an 'ideal beauty' which does not exist. While travelling, I have seen so many beautiful people of all different shapes, colors, and forms, and I reflect this beauty, likewise, in my designs."

She prefers to create a design dictated by the body of the woman it is designed for and not the other way around, with the goal of making that woman feel beautiful in the female body that is uniquely hers. Many of her pieces have caught the eye of performers who are looking for clothes that are not only exquisitely tailored, but mirror their individual style and passion for life.

Dreamy colors are knitted and woven into light, soft, lacy garments to be layered and mixed, heavy on texture but lightweight in multicolored yarns.

WUTHIGRAI SIRIPHON,
Bangkok, Thailand

less distraction by a riot of color can really draw attention into pure consciousness of texture, either in the pattern created by the weave or knit construction of a fabric itself, or in a texture created by braiding, beading, embroidering, knotting, smocking, pleating, twisting, or seaming. Be it boldly stated or understated, multicolored and patterned or not, texture sings its song of touch, weight, and movement.

Texture may attract visually, first, but the very next impulse is to reach out and touch what is seen. To delight with texture is to create luxury of form that wants to be handled, and texture should always be the

Rows of sequins add bulk, texture, and directional pattern to this wrap top and straight skirt ensemble. The skirt runs sequins across, covered by a thin layer of organza for smoothness. The top, uncovered, crosses the bodice on bias and falls in sculptural folds and bends due to its weight.

Illustration: LAURA VOLPINTESTA,
New York, NY, USA
Ensemble: PATACHOU, BELO HORIZONTE,
Minas, Brazil

Even in a single color, this outfit's textures would tell a story. The tailored matte wool suiting cape has a silky reflective lining. The fine-gauged knit sweater features a tall, ribbed-waistline, shiny matelasse skirt of an organic horizontal pattern over Lycra leggings in a coated finish for lots of sensory stimulation in celebratory colors.

AGATHA RUIZ
DE LA PRADA,
Madrid, Spain

benefit of the wearer's experience inside the clothes as well. Linings, seam finishes, and the "wrong" side of any fabric affect the wearer's experience inside the textural aspects of the clothes.

Extremely fine and fluid, airy and light fabrics are as textural as any other. There is a tendency to refer to heavy-textured garments as textured; each type exists only in relation to the other. All fabrics have textures, and the treatments we use to create garments also create textures, like a gathered waist, quilting, a drawstring, a row of buttons, bones, stitches, or cowls.

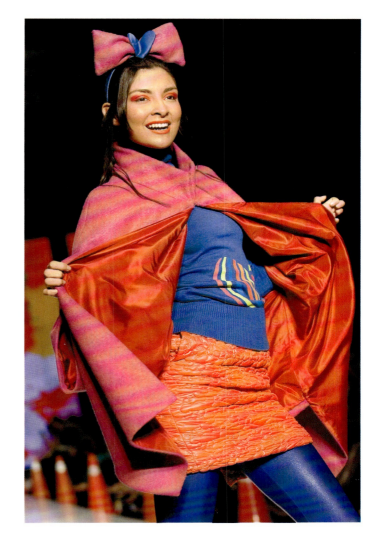

Inspired by nature, and using her imagination, Eva Soto Conde created this eye-catching asymmetrical bird silhouette to explore the behavior and finishing technique on various textiles and inform an amalgam of various textural rhythms, patterns, and sizes.

EVA SOTO CONDE,
Madrid, Spain

print \ 'print \ *n*

1: A mark or impression made in or on a surface by pressure **b:** The pattern itself. **5:** A design or picture transferred from an engraved plate, wood block, lithographic stone, or other medium.

18

A piece of art in itself, a print should be able to stand alone. In two dimensions, color, and shape come together in endless manifestations. A print is applied to fabric. Patterns and weaves such as stripes and plaids can be imitated by printing

PHOTO: WANDERINGBRUMMELL.COM

them on a garment, but if they are woven in, then they just aren't prints.

One way to recognize a print is that the "wrong side" of the garment does not carry the pattern. Some fabric-printing techniques and fabrics, however, will show very little or no difference at all between the right and wrong side, which opens up a wider range of options for their use and finishing techniques. But, generally, the printed fabric has a "right" and a "wrong" side.

Potato print, block print, and sun print are some age-old techniques for applying motifs to fabrics. If the plate or block is
(continued on page 151)

This street shot captures a beautiful moment, featuring a high-contrast print in a complementary color story.

AMRIT JAIN,
WANDERING BRUMMEL,
Denhi, India

Diane von Furstenberg

NEW YORK

Diane von Furstenberg was born Diane Simone Michelle Halfin on December 31, 1946, in Brussels, Belgium, and raised in Europe and Scandinavia. Her mother, a concentration camp survivor, is said to have given her daughter a deep sense of self-worth, tenacity, and strength that is visible in her style and business. At twenty years old, she married a prince, and in 1969 she moved to New York City from Italy, gave birth to her daughter Tatiana, and started to make samples of her designs. She was very active in the social and artistic scenes in New York, including Studio 54.

In 1972, she started her own manufacturing business, making a hit with a sweater dress named "Angela" after the black activist Angela Davis. Then she launched her iconic jersey wrap dress, and by 1976 she had sold 5 *million* wrap dresses! A symbol of the feminine liberation of the times, it was sexy yet professional, affordable, comfortable, beautiful, flattering, and adaptable to day and evening.

In 1983, she divorced, her business crashed, and she moved back to Europe and started a publishing house. In the early 1990s, she designed a line for QVC called Silk Assets and moved back to the United States. She published her autobiography, *Diane: A Signature Life,* about her fashion career and marriage. She restarted her now-thriving business in 1997, brought back by demand as shoppers pulled her clingy dresses out of vintage shops in testament to their relevance to women's needs again.

Today, she is known both for her designs and the design of her business model. She believes in lean inventory and intelligent, accessible pricing. President of the Council of Fashion Designers of America,

she is highly respected, influential, and philanthropic in her business. She told the *New York Times* that she advises young designers to grow their businesses naturally, rather than wish to be bought by big companies, so that they can be in control of their growth and form.

Producing garments that are timeless, elegant, and practical, DVF is a private, family business, with thirty-one boutiques. Her clothes exude confidence and personality, travel well, and are durable, affordable, and luxurious. Von Furstenberg's sense of color, graphics, and print development is highly evolved and unapologetic. The spirit is feminine, independent, active, and vivacious. She designs passionately as a woman for women. Her company is 97 percent female, including its president, and she hopes that her granddaughter may take over the business one day. The flagship store in New York is in the same building as her penthouse apartment and headquarters, integrating her life with her work.

Her philanthropic work includes the DVF Awards, since 2010, which awards $50,000 to recipients exhibiting leadership and courage in efforts for women's causes. She also supports numerous international organizations related to design, women's health (breast cancer, AIDS), business, children, and families.

Batik, woven, two-color and directional, mini or maxi, but always distinctive, print plays a principal role in Diane von Furstenberg's collections. Black and white are often used, if not strongly contrasting flat color values, to crisply pop the pattern's attributes as the developed concepts carry the color story for each collection. Interacting with the viewer, the body, and the garment's cut lines, the arts of print and fashion design mingle on a highly sophisticated level in her hands. From collection to collection, she works with different levels of hardness and softness in the fabrics and prints to offer a range of experiences, but the print always carries a strong effect.

Layered camouflage over an improvised silk camouflage breaks the pattern into textured and solid organic shapes, with intention to layer and mix.

TOMMY HILFIGER,
New York, NY, USA

Mixed silk scarf patterns use bordered and placement prints that emphasize the square pattern of each panel, mixing motifs in brilliant patterns and colors for a random, kaleidoscopic effect in peasant tops and full skirts for romance mixed with luxury.

D&G, BY DOLCE AND GABBANA,
Milan, Italy

These sundrenched, large-scale, geometric prints are entirely integrated into each dress design and can't be cut randomly. Pattern pieces are strategically placed precisely onto the patterned fabric. The style of print is the designer's hallmark.

MARA HOFFMAN,
New York, NY, USA

durable, then there is the possibility of repetition, reusing the printing medium again and again. In the industrial era, prints were designed to repeat seamlessly, from the smallest pattern on a calico or polka dot, to the outstanding and often megasized motifs on Dutch Wax prints made for the African fashion market. Print design rose to new levels of artistry.

Using small-scale, artisanal methods (obviously more precious, unique, and labor intensive) or the newest high-speed mass production technologies, prints delight and converse with wearers and observers. They can tell stories to children or adults, reflect

The print features only multicolored women's faces and hairstyles in a distinctive, allover graphic print.

Z-SPOKE, BY ZAC POSEN,
New York, NY, USA

This pair uses two geo-prints developed by the designer, who highly develops her textiles each season. One has softer tones in a larger-scale motif, the other features a wider range of tones and values, including black. The print is intentionally cut, pleated, joined, and manipulated to play with rhythm and visual effects. Part plan, part improvisation.

FERNANDA YAMAMOTO,
São Paulo, Brazil

A print that starts from a solid edge is gradually broken into white by a flying bird motif. This engineered print repeats only horizontally, using just three colors in a vibrant vintage feel that becomes the designer's trademark. Trims add to the color palette.

NORMA AND HENRY,
BY LEAH CAHILL,
Frenchtown, NJ, USA

NORMA & HENRY/A-LINE SKIRTS BY LEAH CAHILL

values, carry slogans, pronounce membership in a group or subculture, perpetuate history and cultural traditions, shock, inspire, dream, control, liberate, blend, romance, cheer, dress up, and dress down.

A print can have as few as two colors, or even just a shiny resin on a solid ground. Inkjet printing is making endless colors and combinations possible without the use of cylinders or blocks. New technology makes it easy to recolor and change the positions of colors in an existing print. Paintings can be manipulated to become repeating patterns. The repeat may be visible or undetectable, or have an obvious or notable border running through it.

Screen-print logos, artwork, and motifs are modern society's billboards as well as mass-produced art-to-wear and identity markers. Licensed characters, messages, and brand names call out to us from garments every day. Prints have scale in relation to one another, and to the body. Endless creativity and innovation ensues, for as long as clothing exists. A designer can express so much in a garment, and a universe can be expressed in the raw material, or a printed fabric.

This pair of design illustrations uses Vlisco Dutch Wax cotton prints in maxi and mini scale, coordinated by the house of Vlisco and blocked together by the designer. Gouache and Sharpie Illustration.

LAURA VOLPINTESTA,
New York, NY, USA

con·trast \ kn-trst, kntrst \ *v*

1: To set in opposition in order to show or emphasize differences.

19

What is fashion, if not contrast? Contrast is everywhere in fashion: body types, silhouettes and shapes, variations in color, texture, attitude, movement, edge, culture, style. Contrast in design creates energy.

If a garment's impact is in its details, however many or few, it is in contrast to other parts that a detail is noticed. Most notably in use of color, texture, or silhouette (cinched waist, wide shoulder), contrast creates a tiny ripple or a tidal wave of excitement, an a-ha moment of surprise that pulls you deeper into the designer or wearer's process of telling a unique story.

Contrasts form a relationship between things because of their difference. Wide versus narrow, curved versus straight, busy versus quiet, dark versus light, day-into-evening, plain versus busy. These pairings, these (continued on page 158)

This soft shell of a dress with gently draped, cuffed sleeves and an asymmetrical, curved decorative layer in front can be left flat or belted back to expose the panel's contrast underside.

DISAYA COLLECTION, BY DISAYA SORAKRAIKITIKUL, *Bangkok, Thailand*

Duro Olowu

LONDON

Picture bold, tailored shapes with clean lines and edges in firm fabrics, paired with fluid, bias, color-blocked, and mixed-pattern separates and gowns with strong silhouettes and distinct patterns of all kinds, brought together with a distinct sensibility. These are the makings of a Duro Olowu design.

Duro Olowu was born in Nigeria and raised in Lagos. His Jamaican mother used to find local tailors to create shirts and home goods made from local fabrics, combined with fabrics she collected abroad, which was an influence on his view of fabrics and colors. Many are speaking of mixing print as a trend, but in African culture, "This is not a trend, it is an art," according to Olowu, who offers this abundantly in his designs. A subtle and overt language of interacting prints forms the core of an artist's and a wearer's world, not only for a season.

The patterns and colors of his designs, which are sold around the world to concept stores like Ikram in Chicago and Biffi in Milan, may seem African. Yet Olowu's fabrics are often British-made prints of his own design or Italian, French, or Swiss fabrics that reflect this African heritage and world travels. He describes himself as a multicultural fashion designer with an international worldview. He lives and works in both London and New York.

His signature printed dresses caught the attention of U.S. and British *Vogue*, winning New Designer of the Year in 2005 at the British Fashion Awards. He brings together London and Lagos in his design, most notably the mixing of imported and local styles, layering contrasting graphic prints for visual rhythm and effect, tailoring, and long-skirted silhouettes, all com-

monly found in west African dress. He sees dressing well as a source of pride and is fascinated by the fact that fabric tells a story. His garments bring together fabrics from all over the world.

He makes a distinct point of using models from all over the world, because, he says, it makes a statement about "what you want from the world" and enhances the beauty and appeal of his aesthetic. He also believes that his designs need to travel well.

JCPenney is featuring him as a seasonal designer for 2013 to help revamp their image. He is embracing the opportunity to make his pricey pieces available to the masses and explore the democratic aspect of American fashion, while giving it a global slant. Underneath it all, he wants to give the woman garments that nurture "inner beauty and joy."

Double-faced wool in light and dark values manipulates contrasting surfaces and shapes. From rounded forms and angular, flat planes are blocked out in a bold, flat surface and color.

ANA LOCKING,
Madrid, Spain

relationships, inspire and ignite a flame. Recognizing contrast in a garment or group's design may be startlingly obvious (dramatically oversized pockets, contrast color trim on a solid dress, bulky embellishments), but contrasts can also be intimate secrets, such as the case of a lining used in an unexpected color or print, or a garment that looks rigidly structured or professional but is unbelievably comfortable and easy to wear. Contrast can be found in associations: a day fabric for evening or symbolic adornments from a culture or subculture brought into unexpected social settings. Contrasting juxtapositions can be visual (the high shine of metallic

Trim ruffles border the flared layers of this swinging tiered dress and the asymmetrical shoulder cap with an accent of pattern reminiscent of seed bead embroidery without the weight. The same print is used for an overall dress at right, with solid contrast trim.

ISABELA CAPETO,
Rio de Janeiro, Brazil

This cotton blazer challenges and surprises, with ikat fabric applied to the jacket hem in usage typical of lace. Cutting into an area that pulls an unexpected floral motif out of the traditionally geometrical pattern (compare to the lining), the designer finds a scalloped edge, also lacelike. The jacket lining is a denser, nude-toned ikat designed for the owner's secret pleasure. Every component of the garment is patterned and contrasted subtly with creamy colors.

FROU FROU,
BY G. ARCHANA RAO,
Hyderabad, India

sequins against a wool tweed or jersey) or tactile (a fluid silk paired with crisp, firm taffeta).

Even the skin color of the wearer can become a basis for contrast. A designer can create "nude" tones that are similar to the wearer's skin tones for a nude effect or use colors that intentionally strike off the skin tone to draw attention to either the garment or the wearer, depending on that designer's sensibility.

Design that contrasts with our preconceived ideas about what should and should not happen in a garment (as in deconstruction), that looks to rebel or to inspire the delight of discovery, that wakes up society and shakes up the status quo, can make us ask questions or reexamine values. Examples are the first designers to take away corsets, or to see distressed garments as more valuable than "perfect" protected ones.

Contrast comes from lining cowl-draped pockets with complementary-colored lining from the pastel palette. The single-toned, metallic-finish knit top echoes the cowl with its draped collar.

IGGY POPOVIC ATELIER,
BY IGGY GIORGOS POPOUKS,
Zagreb, Croatia

di·rec·tion \ dih-rek-shuhn \ *n*
2: The line along which anything lies, faces, moves, with reference to the point or region toward which it is directed.

20

The raw material of most garments is traditionally woven or knit. Both of these structures have distinct linear grains that flow along the length of the fabrics. Known as the true grain, this basic structural reality of its fabrication is usually considered

in the design and construction of any piece. Even when pattern pieces are already designed, the way they are laid out on the raw material needs to respect the grain and consider the fabric's behavior and how the pieces will fit between its borders before cutting.

In patterned fabrics, repeated motifs or weaves, stripes, or prints across the length of the fabric take on a flow that is usually undeniable. While some fabrics are actually designed to be directionally resistant, such as tiny, scattered florals or tossed polka dots, other fabrics can intentionally take on (continued on page 164)

The horizontals, verticals, and diagonals in primary colors against a neutral black/beige ground in this outfit are taken one step further when emphasized with micro ruffles of tasseled fringed trim, for an earthy feel. Perhaps the most delightful elements are the center front button placket, curving around just below the waist, and the cutaway jacket exposing nonmatched stripes in the skirt, taking the ordered chaos up a notch.

ANNA SUI,
New York, NY, USA

The dress at right has straight-grain straps and midriff, while other components of both looks are constructed on the true bias, made evident by the clear orientation of the plaid fabric. Claire McCardell's garments are as functional, relevant, and beautiful today as they were sixty years ago. Notice the straight grain edges cut into zigzag necklines which integrate the fabric and design.

Claire McCardell

© GENEVIEVE NAYLOR/CORBIS

McCardell's designs paved the way for what we consider American design—functional, practical, wearable, work-and-play clothes that innovate and solve problems. Her daywear moved into evening. Her tent dresses came with spaghetti strap belts that the wearer could adjust for the perfect fit and silhouette.

Claire McCardell (American, 1905–1958) is a definitive early icon of modern American sportswear. She stepped into the fashion scene when World War II restrictions made French fabrics and fashions unavailable, so she used what she could come by, which included wool jersey and denim, incorporating plaids and stripes. This also was the birth of uniquely American design. Her wartime frugality and sparing use of humble, affordable fabrics and cuts to create timeless silhouettes made her an early adapter of sustainable principles. Because of this, her clothes were mass-produced in the United States at very affordable prices.

Reflecting the times, her fashions included the "popover dress," a denim wrap dress that could be worn over dress clothes, like an apron, during the era that domestic help was not affordable; the monastic, a bias-cut, tentlike dress that could be worn with or without a belt; the "diaper suit" and cotton halter-top gowns for evening. These iconic creations evolved into various incarnations throughout her career. McCardell's styles offered casual sophistication and practicality to women.

Rather than darting the bodice with restricting cuts, her bias shapes skimmed over the upper body, liberated the shoulders for movement, and draped generously around it.

Aiming to design modern clothes that could travel, McCardell launched a six-piece collection of coordinated separates in 1934. Sports clothing inspired her creations: bathing suits in wool jersey, leotards, and clothes for golf, skiing, and cycling.

She used shaped sleeves to enhance the shoulders through the cut without padding and used spaghetti ties and large patch pockets in many of her designs. The shirtdress, tomboy, black jersey leggings, and hooded anoraks were all iconic looks for her. The play of stripes and plaids is evident in many of her garments, exposing the bias cuts. Her clothes often had loose shapes with adjustable belts or drawstrings or bias stretch that made them adaptable to a range of body types.

Avoiding darts and complex construction created affordable, elegant, innovative modern design for women's lifestyles. She introduced the ballet flat during tight shoe rationing during the war, often in fabric matching the outfit. Her winter wear often included hoods for warmth, and she introduced wool for evening.

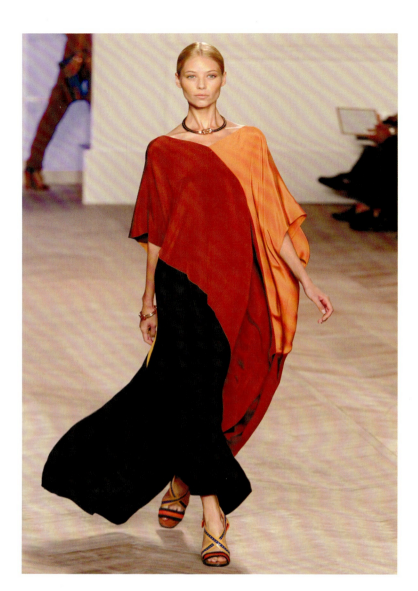

direction in their artwork, either featuring a motif that cannot be cut "upside down" or by repeating with a definitive flow. These features must be considered when a designer chooses or creates a patterned fabric for a garment.

Finally, even in solid, nongrained fabrics, a design can use seams or edges that take on energetic direction with flowing lines. Applied embellishments, screen prints, or logos can also carry a sense of movement and direction, so that when direction is present in a garment, even a fitted, firm garment with no excesses can still carry a sense of flow or dramatic movement. This kind of flair moves energy, and energy is life, so direction is another way to breathe life into a garment, even before someone puts it on.

This highly directional print, joined by solid white triangles and white-bordered triangles of print, is a testament to the dynamic energy of triangles. For extra pop, each triangle-shaped panel features the print pointing in a different direction.

MARTIN LAMOTHE,
London, UK/Barcelona, Spain

Bold, vibrant colors in high-contrast, large-scale, directional prints layer volume, one direction over the other. A cutaway jacket reveals the results.

RONALDO FRAGA,
Belo Horizonte, Miras, Brazil

FIRSTVIEW.COM

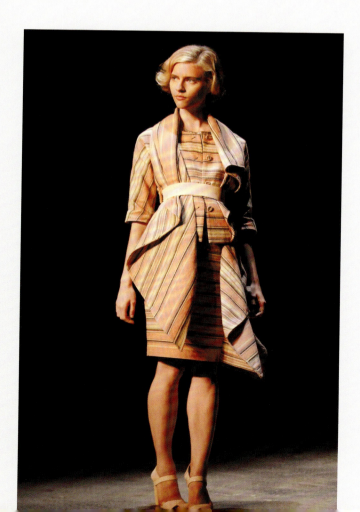

Yarn-dyed woven stripes run cut on the cross grain for a basic top and skirt. Excess fabric cascades down the skirt and jacket fronts on purpose in a play of angles that separates the look into directional changes. Sleeves are cut on bias for a softer visual effect than the horizontal stripe.

TIA CIBANI,
Vancouver, Canada

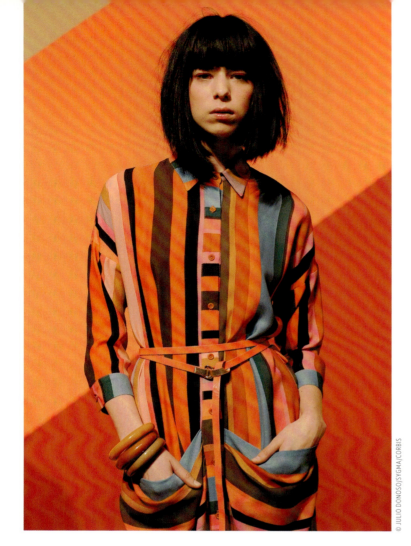

© JULIO DONOSO/SYGMA/CORBIS

The oblique blocked background is the clincher: A tunic shirtdress cut from nonrepeating vertical broad striping is divided by a horizontally cut center front placket. Suddenly, the fabric takes on a very different rhythm when cut only an inch wide at the placket and punctuated by red shirt buttons. Horizontal belting is solid, sleeves are cuffed as a contrasting color, and huge pockets also use the stripe crosswise, but intentionally not blending with the placket, for an overall collision of direction.

COREY LYNN CALTER,
Los Angeles, CA, USA

This large but delicate motif takes a strong orientation up the cleanly constructed center front panel, avoiding the in-seam pockets, and echoes up the sleeves. The same motif takes a horizontal orientation at the hem, changing direction and filling the A-lined silhouette's hem with pattern. The pattern is cut off each time it reaches a seam or neckline, while carefully centered on each pattern piece.

FRANCIS MONTESINOS,
Valencia, Spain

This truly directional graphic print flows undeniably and energetically upward (not downward) and to the left in the skirt, while an enormous cowl changes direction completely from the waist up, for dynamic movement and change of path, all achieved with minimal cut.

CAROLINA HERRERA,
New York, NY, USA

Highly directional stripes with zigzag edges and shine carry the eye upward and across these looks, shaped without violating the stripe with darts or seams, matching at armholes (right) and driving along the body's curves with subtle shape and high energy.

MARÍA ESCOTÉ,
Barcelona, Spain

em·bel·lish·ment \ em-bel-ish-muhnt \ *n*
1: an ornament or decoration.

21

A garment is cut, fit, and finished. Embellishment denotes a last step, a finishing touch, an extra, yet not without prior consideration.

Since the beginning of history, decoration comes after the essential step of creating the base

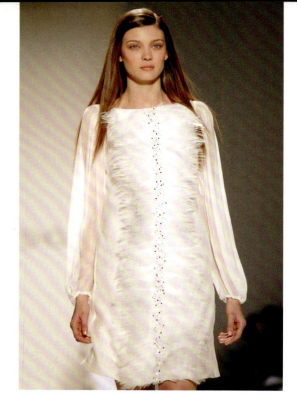

garment except where decorative adornments, and not garments, were the only form
of body decoration.

In fashion, a base garment may exist
only for the purpose of carrying the ornament, or inversely an ornament is applied to
a finished garment, calling attention to itself
as it lures the eye, then settling into the overall look. Embellishment is the punctuation
mark of fashion design, the icing on the cake.
Many embellishments walk a line between
jewelry and garment. Jewelry can add interest or break up the symmetry of a garment
and can be used interchangeably,
(continued on page 172)

**This simple white dress
carries delicate vertical
beading bordered by
horizontal white feathers
symmetrically down center
front, almost like a soft
armor. Simply, naturally, the
monochromatic embellish-
ment is primarily textural.**

TADASHI SHOJI,
*Tokyo, Japan/Los Angeles,
CA, USA*

In 1988, Patrick Kelly became the first American
designer inducted to the Chambre Syndicale du
Prêt-á-Porter sponsored by Sonia Rykiel and
Yves Saint Laurent. Though his life was cut short,
in 1990 after eight seasons in four years, he is
remembered as one of fashion's greats. His flamboyant, fresh, and feminine design perspective
often used embellishment with buttons and ribbons as part of its language, along with hats and
fun accessories, celebrating his rural southern
African-American roots and the women he grew
up with. He noted, "At the Black Baptist church
on Sunday, the ladies are just as fierce as at
the Yves Saint Laurent couture shows." He was
also a well-known collector of Black Americana
and created images that brought controversial
racial stereotyping up for discussion, while celebrating his roots.

Kelly's cultural background made him a
unique voice in Paris. His first big hit in Paris
was a collection that featured body-hugging,
bright-colored, and elegant jersey minidresses
adorned with colorful buttons. The Brooklyn
Museum held the first, sixty-piece retrospective
of his work in 2004, and many of his garments
are in museum collections.

Born in 1954, he grew up in Vicksburg, Mis-
sissippi. As a young person, his female relatives
influenced him strongly with their common
practice of adding embellishments to store-
bought garments to make them unique. His
mother taught him to draw, and his grandmother, who taught him to sew, worked as a domestic
in an affluent household and would bring home
fashion magazines. When Kelly lost buttons on
his clothes as a boy, his mother would replace
them with a mismatching button, and then pep-
per the rest of the garment with buttons to dis-
tract from the fact that it didn't match (and create a design). He described them as full-figured
women, and professed to design for all body
types, big and small, "real-woman" proportions.

Patrick Kelly

NEW YORK

In young adulthood, he lived in Atlanta, selling recycled clothes and dressing windows at the Yves Saint Laurent Rive Gauche boutique, before moving to New York to attend Parsons School of Design.

In the mid-to-late 1980s, Kelly launched himself in Paris, first by selling dresses on the street and working as a costumer for a nightclub, sewing up hundreds of dresses. Occasionally, he would hold guerrilla-style fashion shows on the street with his Black model friends wearing his dresses. He and his life and business partner Bjorn Aleman presented his dresses to the Victoire boutiques in 1984, who offered to produce and carry his line of dresses and referred him to French *Elle*, who then featured him in a six-page spread in February 1985. This was unheard of for an unknown designer, and Victoire had never carried an American designer before. His flamboyant clothes became well known and got the attention of Warnaco after Bette Davis wore one of his dresses on the David Letterman show in 1987 and announced that her designer friend was looking for financial backing.

Soon Henri Bendel, Bloomingdale's, and Bergdorf Goodman were carrying his Paris designs, with icons such as Isabella Rossellini, Goldie Hawn, Jessie Norman, Farrah Fawcett, Madonna, Cicely Tyson, Princess Diana, and Grace Jones, among others wearing his fashions. After his summer 1987 collection was released, he moved into his own showroom and produced his clothes by Ghinea in Bologna. His iconic ad campaigns were very distinctive and lively, featuring himself and a lineup of models all dressed in his clothes.

depending on the mood or occasion, or even combine with different looks for different effects. Embellishments, however, carry a much higher level of commitment, staying with the garment, becoming an intrinsic part of the design, and so deserve careful consideration. The creativity in embellishment becomes the designer's choice and the wearer's agreement to carry.

Trims and notions are often used as embellishments: buttons, eyelet ruffle, beaded fringe by the yard, ribbons, beads, sashes, patches, crystals, zippers, and so on.

Embellishments can showcase fine handcrafts beyond dressmaking and tailoring techniques, using them in new or surprising ways. Beading, embroidery, fabric flowers, smocking, and pleating, for example, call attention to a garment's detail or carry a story or message. Embellishing always indicates extra effort for the wearer's preciousness.

New technology and materials also bring new possibilities and trends of embellishment—nailheads and heat-fused crystals and beads, for example—while the conventional notions take on new personalities in a designer's creative hands. Even a sash or twist of fabric, coordinating brooch, or contrast screen-print motif becomes an embellishment

With richness and luxury, the woman's preciousness is enveloped in painstaking decoration from top to bottom, as each layer of craft blends into the next, fading out into sheer silk at hem. From geometric to natural, crystal-hard to soft, light to dark, the dress is a canvas for a skilled artisan, in the woman's honor, without overpowering her.

PRABAL GURUNG,
New York, NY, USA

A sprinkling of sparkly
studs comes off the punk
leather jacket and onto
a clean, neutral cropped
shrug. The irregular metallic
bars woven into the sheer
blouse feel more like applied
embellishment than a
standard repeat pattern.

CAROLINA HERRERA,
New York, NY, USA

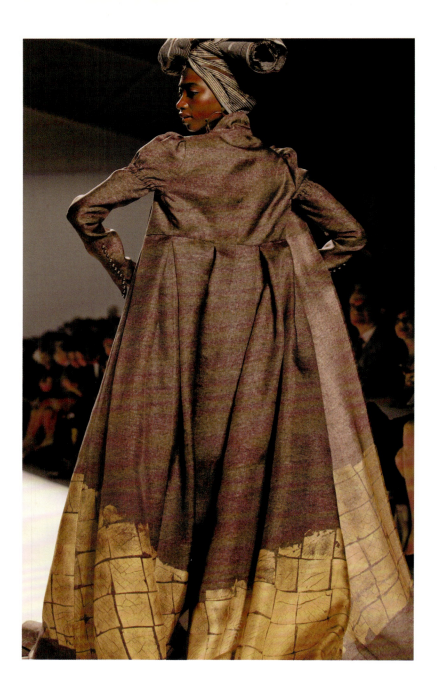

if it is applied to the garment with the intention to stay and serves a purpose of calling attention to an area of the garment with complexity, contrast, or other interest.

A particular philosophy toward embellishment usually becomes part of a designer's unique trademark sensibility, rarely used by minimalists, usually adding to the complexity of a design. Embellishment traditionally made the wearer seem more important because nonessential decoration is an excess and a luxury, even if it is also a basic human need often overlooked or priced out in mass production.

Today, with deconstruction, the category has expanded to include safety-pinned rips and tears in denim, unfinished, distressed fabrics, or even pieces of recycled garments cut and applied out of context. Bleaching a

Layered over a matching fitted strapless pantsuit, a flowing tent jacket in a natural texture with a generous hem is embellished with fine rows of sleeve buttons and hand-painted gold blocks that dress it up.

ZANG TOI,
New York, NY, USA

Saturated primary hues and gold are scattered over a black ground in a print that plays with the idea of embellishment. The random pattern of the precious jewelry motif is cut off by garment seams and closures. Though it is entirely two dimensional, the print has a heavy, chunky feel.

OSCAR DE LA RENTA,
*Dominican Republic/
New York, NY, USA*

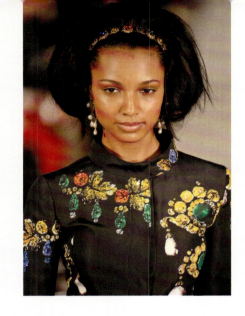

garment and then ripping out the hem seam can create a beautiful textured border in the original color.

Using notions and trims just scratches the surface of the concept of embellishment and where it can go. While accessories like jewelry give more freedom in personalizing a look because they can be added or subtracted or interchanged with garments at will, embellishments involve a level of commitment by the wearer and the designer to have a lasting integration with the design for life.

Is it embellishment or construction? A little bit of both, when swags of contrast white chiffon are pleated into the armhole, drawing the eye up, and draped across the bustline of a sheath dress, where they can be tied or left trailing; constructed, but not necessary to the dress's shaping. Three rows of beaded embellishments are bold and reminiscent of a triple-breasted jacket closure, but their subdued tones take second stage to the white sashes.

TRACY REESE,
New York, NY, USA

pat·tern \ pat-ern; British pat-n \ *n*
a: An artistic or decorative design

22

Across the design of a collection, the designer may be working out a pattern of garment shapes that interact logically with each other. Pattern is never associated with the random or accidental; pattern joins with that part of human nature that

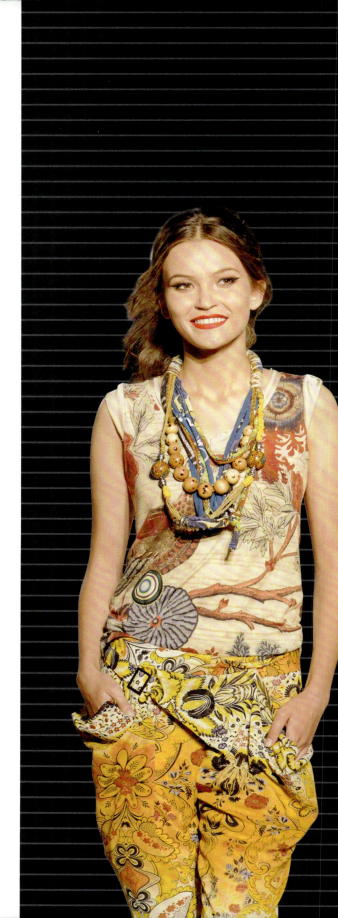

looks for logic, recognizes repetition, and is comforted by order.

A fabric design, in order to cover larger quantities of fabric easily whether hand stamped or industrially printed, will use a repeating block to create a pattern that expands endlessly across lengths and widths of fabric. At some point, that design pattern repeats, however subtly or overtly.

A row of buttons, pin tucks, a series or repetition of pleats, ruffles, or beads on a garment become a pattern whether intentionally or not, as like parts are grouped together visually. A single pattern can "flatten *(continued on page 180)*

In illustrating patterns or prints, whether large or small in scale, it is important to consider the size of the motif in relation to the human body in order to render it to the scale and repeat that it would have on the figure, and not the size it is on the swatch itself, for accuracy. Here, an illustration with the accompanying swatch.

DESIGN ILLUSTRATION.
LAURA VOLPINTESTA,
New York, NY, USA

Desigual

BARCELONA

Desigual was established in 1983 when Thomas Meyer, of Swiss origin, started designing T-shirts to sell to vacationers in Ibiza, famous for its nightlife. His vision was of fun, affordable, spirited clothing. He made a bomber jacket out of recycled blue jeans that was so successful he had to make a name for his company, Desigual, with the slogan "It's Not the Same." This name is fused with the expansive philosophy that focuses on individuality, sharing opinions, and embracing differences. Valuing growth, innovation, tolerance, and positivism, Desigual designs clothing to "make their customers fall in love," to elicit emotion and evoke enthusiasm, and fill the streets with their happy vision.

The brand grew in popularity but needed to restructure its business and marketing or shut its doors by the onset of the 1990s. Desigual focused on the Spanish market, including a central location in Barcelona and stores like its original in three tourist resorts; did runway shows; and launched a website. During this time, a strong relationship with the customer was established, as well as a period of improving product quality and production processes.

To this day, the vision of the company (which employs twenty-five designers) is stated clearly not only in its aesthetic but in all of its press and marketing. The company believes that work and fun should go together. Desigual, like its name, strives to stand out and proclaims to dress "people, not bodies"—people who love what they do and live life fully.

Thomas Meyer started designing his own original, graffiti-inspired prints early on and befriended Manel Adell (who would lead Desigual to great success in the new

millennium). In early 2000, Adell came on as CEO until 2012, and with Marti Guixe started the concept of painting parties, which led to the work of customers and friends to be used to decorate their stores. This publicity brought more and more popularity to the brand. Childrenswear was launched in 2004, and in 2005, twenty-four new stores were launched, along with a daring new campaign called "Naked: Enter half-nude, leave dressed for free," in which a certain number of customers who arrived first in their undergarments would leave the store fully dressed. This campaign was explosively popular, starting in Spain. In 2006, Desigual started to branch out beyond the Spanish market and launched the Naked campaign in Portugal, London, Berlin, Stockholm, Madrid, and New York in 2010. Three hundred shoppers lined up outside the New York store in their undergarments. Such promotions have helped make Meyer a billionaire.

In 2011, Desigual worked on a line with the equally exuberant Christian Lacroix and also started a long-term collaboration with Cirque du Soleil, creating sixty garments and accessories to be sold both at Desigual stores and Cirque du Soleil show boutiques. Currently selling in eighty countries and employing 3,000 people from seventy-two countries, Desigual has 275 of its own shops.

Now focusing on Mexico, Brazil, and Europe, the brand continues to grow and expand in popularity and has strong design philosophy backed with corporate social responsibility policies, adhering to core values that fuse the lifestyle and aesthetic that set the brand apart.

This illustration featuring a circular graphic print is cut at the empire waist, causing an interesting interruption in the pattern. Notice how the single graphic geometric pattern "flattens" the dress, bringing all of the pattern to the front. Contrast linear pattern in a complementary color punctuates the hemline.

JACQUELINE HELOISE,
Burlington, VT, USA

out" visually, while patched and mixed patterns cognitively are interpreted as multilayered.

Fashion garment patterns such as the sleeve, bodice, skirt, and so on, have the power to repeat as they are traced and reproduced as often as needed, as well as modified at any time to create a specifically shaped new pattern.

Patterns have a specific shape and form that are recognizable, independent of their style or aesthetic. Floral, geometric, abstract, naturally derived, woven or knitted, hand stitched, screen printed, or heat creased, there is pattern in the garment. Personal or mandated, overt or subtle, pattern is a mode of expression that shows up in everything we wear. Textiles themselves are woven or knitted with lines or loops that in themselves create pattern, however fine or bulky. Single-colored fabrics may be richly woven in textural jacquard, flocking, burnout, openwork, eyelet, loops, or reflective yarns. Notions such as ribbons, yarns, threads, even buttons and elastics can be applied or inserted in such a way that results in a patterned effect.

Though not explicit in its definition, pattern carries a rhythmic or temporal connotation. A single motif may blare out from

Pattern-blocked bias and straight-grain panels in contrasting floral patterns are edged with small-scale geometrical bias binding in an energetic harmony creating a pattern.

NICOLE MILLER,
New York, NY, USA

Shapes of contrast color create linear and curved graphic effects, as well as visual and textural pattern in a balanced play of positive and negative in this knitted garment.

KRIZIA ROBUSTELLA,
Barcelona, Spain

Fine-gauge and heavyweight heather and heather varie-gated yarns mix patterns, weights, and transparency in layered knit and crochet.

ANN YEE,
New York, NY, USA

Repeating ruffles, lacing, insets, stripes, and print motifs collide for a riot of colliding patterns softened by gentle dynamics of color value through the grayscale.

AILANTO, BY INAKI & AITOR MUÑOZ,
Madrid, Spain

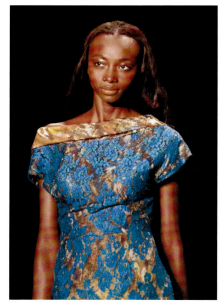

Semisheer floral lace patterns are layered over abstract printed fabrics to create a secondary pattern through their combination.

TIFFANY AMBER, BY FOLAKE FOLARIN-COKER,
Lagos, Nigeria

Three scales of tone and pattern come together in one look: a large graphic coat lining, microbeaded pastel border on a scalloped tiered skirt, and colorful allover pattern of medium-small scale on the blouse.

ALANNAH HILL,
Melbourne, Australia

the center of a gown, or intertwining motifs may weave in and out over its surface twice, thrice, or countless times. The frequency and size of the repetition can take on a motion and speed that are recognized as characteristic of pattern. Perhaps this is its most interesting aspect, because it takes on life as it moves through time.

Fine-scaled, rigid, two-tone patterns over clean shapes define this designer's look and draw attention to clean, precise construction married with geometry, whether the base fabric is fluid or firm.

JUANJO OLIVA,
Madrid, Spain

sur·face \ 'sər-fis \ *n*
a: The outer or the topmost boundary of an object.

surface

23

With fabric as the raw material of fashion and the eyes and skin as interface receptors, surface plays a dual role. Visual and tactile in nature, a surface can seduce the touch, communicate quality, and caress the wearer with its inside. Internal and

external surfaces give two sides to a fashion story. Ideally, nothing is left wanting on either plane. There is nothing worse than wearing an itchy or scratchy, irritating or stifling fabric next to the skin. Fabric selection is the foundation of a design. Even tags, underwires, bones, and closures can be irritating. Quality seam finishes, padding, and linings make a difference on the inside.

Outside surface is functional and aesthetic, while also involving inherent associations connected to the fabric used. Individual taste can dictate the aesthetic interplay of surfaces, but function can play a leading role. (continued on page 188)

Bright colors in reflective hues have more impact when paired with matte shades and smoky layers. Flat wovens, sheers, and built-up, handcrafted textures make these pieces precious and varied.

CELIA VELA,
Barcelona, Spain

Manish Arora's surface interest; innovative, experimental shaping and color; and cultural references and mixes stand out, intentionally. He designs for a woman who wants to be noticed, and he is popular with performing artists and public figures.

Born in India, he graduated from the National Institute of Fashion Technology in New Delhi in 1994 with the "best student" award, going on to launch and show his first collection in 1997. Recognized as India's Rising Star of Indian Fashion, in 2000 he showed at the first India Fashion Week ever, in New Delhi.

In 2001, he launched a diffusion line called Fish Fry, then in 2004 he expanded this to include contemporary sportswear for Reebok. The same year, he was also featured in the exhibit "Global Local" at the Victoria and Albert Museum in London, which focused on the impact of globalization on contemporary Indian design.

Manish admits that his Indian roots give him an edge and capability to do incredible artisanal embroideries, appliqués, beading, and textiles that can only be found in India. He values joy and diversion in fashion and creates fashion for those who don't want to blend into a crowd. At the same time, he says that the aspect of Indian beauty that he most admires is that the women seem unaware of their amazing beauty.

In 2005, he debuted in London Fashion Week, and by 2006, seventy-five stores worldwide were carrying his line. In October 2007, he was invited by Didier Grumbach to show at Paris Fashion Week and collaborated with Japanese, American, and Indian artists to design his collection.

In 2011, Arora was appointed creative director of Paco Rabanne in Paris, for which

Manish Arora

NEW DELHI

he designed two collections. He was recognized as the Clover Group Outstanding Fashion Innovator at the WGSN Fashion Awards 2011.

A lover of fantasy who wants to make people happy, his fashion shows are entertaining, opulent, and outrageous, but his garments are quality pieces, handmade in ateliers in his native India not only for show, but because he also loves craft. He wants his clothes to be functional yet seen as art. His colors may be seen as Indian, but he maintains that regardless of his culture, he is a lover of color.

His unique style is worn by Selena Gomez, Katy Perry, Heidi Klum, Lady Gaga, M.I.A., Britney Spears, and Rihanna, among others. He has also collaborated on many design projects with many labels, including MAC cosmetics, Swatch, dressing the pillars of the Paris Bourse building during Fashion Week spring/summer 2009, Swarovski crystals, chocolates, pastry (for Café de la Paix, Paris), espresso machines, a fiftieth-anniversary Barbie, and an Absolut Vodka dress, among others. He has designed capsule collections for 3 Suisses catalog and Monoprix in France.

Brilliantly colored silks; strong, sculpted silhouettes; and rich hand embroidery are different facets that build Arora's rich, showy aesthetic that blends tradition with innovation.

An analogous color story of unique knits playing with conventions around pattern scale, texture, weight, and opacity pairs with a contrasting knitted pile in a complementary yellow tint.

LYUDMILA NORSOYAN,
Moscow, Russia

A surface has a social connotation for an event or time of day but also has to serve the climate and activity it is chosen for.

Windproofing, waterproofing, stretch, and perforation are some functional aspects that lend a surface to a fabric. Synthetic and natural sources render different effects. Yarns may be soft, napped, slubbed, variegated, furry, flocked, heathered, uneven, crisp, or microdenier. Surfaces may be washable or not. Opacity, reflectivity, and color value all affect play of light on surface. Fabric weight dictates the movement of its fullness when cut. Crisp, fluid, flat, crinkled, knitted, pressed, or washed garments all have

Subdued, fine-textured, hand-drawn, and painted design illustrations contrast with larger, colorful prints created and illustrated digitally, but both collections focus on surface pattern and texture.

GRETA BRADDOCK,
New York, NY, USA

their own way of taking a corner, wrinkling when bent, or behaving on the edge of the silhouette. Surface can affect our perception of a garment as a protective shell, a warm cocoon, an embellished structure, a flag of cheerful color exuberance, or a sculptured drape of alluring chiffon softness.

Analyze surface through its textural feel and visual finish. Is it knitted, felted, woven, crocheted, or knitted? Out of heavy or fine-gauge yarns? Is it beaded, woven, tie-dyed, embroidered, block printed, digital printed, painted on, knit? What is represented in its pattern or motif? Does the surface have an association, such as a shirting, suiting,

Digital inkjet printing yields brilliant colors and expresses the unique voice of the designer by printing her original paintings on fabric in a local facility, opening the field for innovation in surface design.

KATYA LEONOVICH,
Moscow, Russia/New York, NY, USA

Scottish plaid, children's print, Chinese brocade, Indian silk, African print, batik, ikat, day or evening fabric? Is it associated with a gender? Does it represent traditions or new technologies? Does it smell like chemicals, is it sustainable, is it organic, does it breathe, is it recycled or recyclable?

Is it being used the way you are accustomed to seeing it used, or is it a surprise?

Surface is a language that is often taken for granted but is always considered in masterful design.

Like mosaic or collage, the garment is used to unite various pieces of fabrics to delight in the stories they create in color, texture, and panel shapes.

CUSTO BARCELONA,
BY CUSTO DALMAU,
Barcelona, Spain

move·ment \ move-ment \ *n*
a: fine arts; the appearance of motion in painting, sculpture, etc. **2:** a particular manner or style of moving.

24

movement

One of the unique aspects of fashion design compared with other visual arts is that it comes to life on a moving, breathing, human form. This, to the designer or viewer, is a sublime aspect of the art. Fashion lives and moves in its peak moments. It

expresses the soul of the wearer, envelops their body, and accompanies their every action. This is as three-dimensional as design gets! The wearer always chooses garments with consideration of ease of movement for the occasion. An urban lifestyle may require safety, protection, or speed. Garments for special occasions and leisurely lives can take more liberties with details that slow down movement, such as long, full skirts (difficult on stairs) or narrow hems (restricting the movement of the legs), wide-sweeping sleeves (can fall into food, machinery, or workspace), or corsetry (can dig into the skin *(continued on page 197)*

Both the stationary and fluid, moving components of this look, from accessory to gown, twist, scribble, drape, and flow in linear movement around the form.

JULIA DALAKIAN,
Moscow, Russia

Ana Locking

MADRID

Ana Locking was born Ana Gonzales in 1970, in Toledo, Spain. She studied fine arts and painting at the Faculty of Fine Arts in Madrid. She founded Locking Shocking in 1996 with her then partner, working as creative director. They received the L'Oreal Paris Award for the best young spring/summer '03 collection and Marie Claire's Gran Prix de la Moda for the Best National Designer in 2004. They dissolved the label and relationship in 2007.

In 2008, Locking founded her new label, Ana Locking, and with her first collection won the L'Oreal Paris Award for the Best Collection from the Cibeles Madrid Fashion Week.

Locking says you can see what she's experiencing in her life through her designs. It is this emotional perspective that brings a personal level to her concepts. She has done individual collections inspired by a significant breakup, money troubles, a favorite movie, and even the current events in fashion that cast fashion designers in a bad light. Her strong shapes and edges, fine craftsmanship, fabric designs, and embellishments are unique and outstanding.

Depending on what is on her mind and in her heart, she "works it out" in the design of the collection. She isolates herself in her home for a week to design the whole collection, then spends the rest of the season making it real, starting with colors, then all of the material concerns with her team, until the runway show. Confessedly very organized, practical, and methodical, she says the looks appear on the runway in the order that she conceived of them.

There is a strong sense of inner and outer in her work. Outside, there are strong colors and shapes. She develops prints around her theme for the season. For exam-

ple, one collection depicted how the dark side and light must coexist by creating a beautiful, engineered floral liberty print that included insects among the blossoms. Another example featured prints that focus on our "inner beauty." Each print was developed out of microscopic images of blood, muscle, and bone tissue.

Her color, sharp silhouettes, pleating, layers, slits, asymmetry, architecture, and tailoring are easily recognizable, but she values this only together with craftsmanship. Locking candidly admits she couldn't exist without her seamstresses and embroiderers.

Her fine arts background keeps her current in the arts and education, collaborating regularly with different cultural institutions, museums, artistic organizations, and schools. She teaches a course at the CSDMM in Madrid that aims to give form to the student's own identity and style in a capsule collection, without losing sight of the business side of fashion.

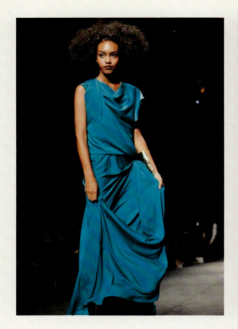

Dynamic pencil sketches emphasize the curve of the spine and flow of the hair and use strong diagonals and curves for maximum movement. It is easy to locate an overall S-curve, or arabesque, in each image.

JAMES HACKETT,
TRINCITY,
Trinidad & Tobago

Ruffles, drapes, and cowls
carry lengths of fabric along
the body like a river to the
sea, pouring out into full,
wide hems in fabrics made
to move.

TUBE GALLERY,
Bangkok, Thailand

and restricts breathing). So movement is a
practical consideration for the wearer.
Movement is an aesthetic consideration as
well, always identified with dynamic, moving
energy, operating on two levels: the physical
and the visual.

Visual movement is easy to recognize
in linear formations. The pure visual and
horizontal are stable and carry movement,
left to right, top to bottom, and vice versa.
Juxtapose the two and there is a collision of
moving energies. Cut into a stripe or line and
add a seam, and you have just interrupted
a movement. The construction of woven or
knit fabric's grains or organization of the mo-

A monochromatic palette
draws attention to the
controlled current of physical
and visual motion of the linear components that release
below the belt.

DAVID TLALE,
Cape Town, South Africa

tifs on a surface pattern lines up as it repeats. Even a nonrepeating motif can have a static or sweeping appearance through curvilinear or geometric forms and edges. The diagonal is the height of movement. A diagonal line feels unpredictable and changing as it travels up and down and across the body simultaneously. All of these properties can be manipulated by designers or wearers when planning a look.

When fashion truly moves in the breeze, flowing around and behind the wearer, softness and drama come into play. The human body is solid and coarse. Many fabrics mimic that shape and form. Fabrics that extend beyond the body seem to blur

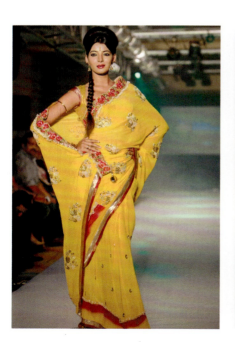

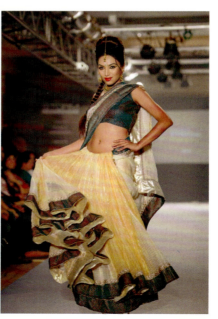

**Ample volumes of flowing
fabric are bordered by heavy
metallic bands that wind
and ripple about the body,
and full hemlines creating
physical and visual movement
embellish both the garment
and the body with flourish
and contrast.**

ANURADHAA BISANI,
Chennai, India

Contrast solid borders, ruffles, lively colorations, directional patterns, fringe, and lace cut in asymmetrical forms keep the eye moving around the body, always discovering something new within the context of traditional fabric types and basic, fitted silhouettes that stabilize, freeing up the surface for improvisation.

CUSTO DALMAU,
FOR CUSTO,
Barcelona, Spain

the boundaries between body and space, between movement and dance, between life and performance, and create forms that "forget" the body for a moment.

Finally, a fashion illustrator uses movement to breathe life into an image. The two-dimensional image represents the living model in the garment, and understanding the visual principles of movement creates excitement and vitality on the paper. The pure vertical plumb line or balance line, balanced by the arabesque or S-curve, with tilting shoulders, pelvis, axis of the head, and diagonal forms in legs and arms, all come together to create movement on the page.

The voluminous sculpture flows into the red accent to form an S-curve, winding from the top of the head to the hem.

ARKADIUS WEREMCZUK,
London, UK

mo·tif \ moh-teef \ *n*
a: a distinctive and recurring form,
shape, figure, etc., in a design

25

While a theme takes on a more abstract connotation that embodies a group, motif speaks of a concrete visual item or symbol that appears in a garment or within a group of looks, often repeating itself exactly or in a variation.

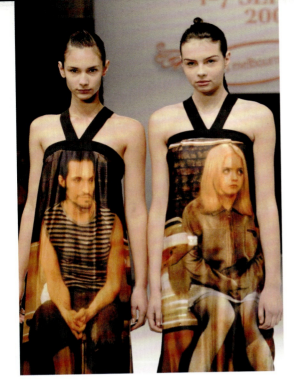

A floral motif, for example, may be beaded onto fabric; heat transferred; hand painted; embroidered; constructed from fabric and attached to the garment; integrated into the seam line formations in the garment; printed or woven repeatedly into the fabric; appear on a button, earring, or shoe; or form hardware on accessories. It may appear in one way or a variety of ways across the concept group.

A motif tends to "speak out" in symbols or forms with associations, identifiable as standing out from a background setting. From abstract forms to realistic, or even (continued on page 205)

Life-size digital prints on this pair of dresses—a motif depicting lifestyle as decoration.

UNIDENTIFIED DESIGNER, MELBOURNE SPRING FASHION WEEK, 2008
Melbourne, Australia

Isabela Capeto

RIO DE JANEIRO

Raffia and shells, sea-foam green, turquoise beading, printed silk, fringe, ruffles, sequins and fabric flowers are played out to form and embellish detailed confections of skilled hand-craft, lively color, and natural texture in a cohesive collection story.

"The fashion business is not as glamorous as it looks. It's hard work." Isabela Capeto said this to a group of students, but you will never find a trace of strain in her beautiful, feminine pieces. Trained at the Accademia di Moda na Itália in Florence, Italy, and now recognized as one of today's most prestigious Brazilian designers, she grew up in a creative house where many things were made by hand. She went on to study industrial design in Rio, while working retail at Zoomp (a major Brazilian designer label), changing her major to visual communication, then social communication. Before becoming her own designer label, Capeto spent some time working in the ateliers of major Brazilian labels such as Maria Bonita, Maria Bonita Extra, and Lenny, as well as having worked with print design for various markets and labels at the house of Bangu.

In April 2003, she finally started her own atelier in Rio de Janeiro and launched her first show for her label in Fashion Rio. She exhibits every six months in show-rooms during Paris Fashion Week in conjunction with Robert Forrest, linking her to the European and Japanese market. She admires Vivienne Westwood's business model of having exclusive pieces available in only a few locations.

Capeto's clothes can be found in more than twenty countries, including Barneys in the United States. After making her debut in Fashion Rio, Capeto was invited with select designers to present her next collection at São Paulo Fashion Week, which is the biggest and most important fashion event in Latin America.

In May 2005, she inaugurated her very first boutique in Rio de Janeiro. Soon after that, in 2006, she opened a second store,

and her small studio moved to a larger and more comfortable space. Currently all the areas, creative, administrative and production, are under the same roof. In 2008, she inaugurated a line for girls between four and ten years old.

She has been carried by Barneys and Jeffrey and was also featured in Macy's "Brasil: A Magical Journey" campaign in 2012, featuring products from her line and also developing pieces exclusively for Macy's. Her aesthetic lies in her approach to developing a collection. Rather than following trends, she looks to museums and books for inspiration, with the point of view that each piece is a work of art. Her designs are elaborate, handmade, always embroidered, dyed, or pleated, with many details such as sequins, antique laces, tulle, ribbons and braids. Capeto's professed objective is to make women feel beautiful wearing romantic clothes. She wants her handmade pieces to create desire. She insists on using domestic fabrics and skilled embroiderers from needy communities in Rio.

She has called attention to herself by launching a lower-priced secondary line, "Ibô" (her childhood nickname and the name of her first label), which uses her excess fabrics from past seasons to create accessories, linings for garments and buttons, even creating an entire girls' line from leftover fabric. Her Ibô label recycles and upcycles to spread the message that creativity is sustainable, proposing looking backward to find solutions for the future. In 2007, the magazine *Imprensa* featured her as one of Brazil's fifty most sustainable companies. Her summer 2010 collection, inspired by the painter Robert Rauschenberg, incorporated fabrics and trims from past collections. Her custom-

ers value that, understanding that reusing material doesn't affect quality, but, in fact, reusing increases value to the ecologically conscious consumer. Finding leftover material an unavoidable reality, she makes a point to integrate it as much as possible into each new collection without disrupting its integrity.

From 2008 to 2011, she became part of the fast-fashion conglomerate Inbrands and learned the hard way that big business can mean fashion loses detail to save money. She aims now to keep her business a small atelier with excellent, limited-production, crafted garments. In a way, she is starting over again now that her company is back in her hands. She rides her bike to work and takes two days a week to personally attend to clients in her store in Rio, calling this "true quality of life, the greatest richness." Her Rio store also has a space that she devotes to carrying other young designers.

photographic, motifs can be appropriated, applied, combined, multiplied, shrunken, expanded, broken, recolored, or crafted however the designer's imagination and production capabilities can work together. Repetition is one of those ingredients that can walk the line between creating a feeling of security, predictability, and safety or tipping the scales into a controlling presence. Seeking balance in the application or integration of motif is an individual journey in dressing or design. One might seek effects that are subtle, secret, repetitive, overt, or bold. Motifs can be read, like a story without words, or can even be words themselves.

Enormously scaled, natural-textured, masculine, metal-hued houndstooth "polka dot" appliqués are shown broken by construction (as they would be if printed) for a clever play of form. Meanwhile, feminine, metal-lic floral, shiny, skintight leggings contrast but tie the look together.

CUSTO BARCELONA,
BY CUSTO DALMAU,
Barcelona, Spain

A zigzag's bold energy gets reinterpreted in varying scales, orientations, and fabrications to create eye-catching garments.

MARIA ESCOTE,
Madrid, Spain

Weaving in and out of view, the motif creates a layer of content within the other layers of a piece such as scale, texture, shape, color, surface, volume, or construction. Motif interacts with each, but always maintains its own body and integrity that makes it a singular, identifiable item, whether spray painted down the front of the jacket or softly profused over a wispy, printed layer of chiffon.

Modern and clean, a very distinct motif repeats across the collection in various color ways, and different neckline design options appeal to personal taste and body type.

JOAQUIN VERDU,
Barcelona, Spain

A yoke-and-fringe construction motif takes on different proportions across the neck and shoulder line but maintains its essential integrity in both manifestations, keeping the concept engaging.

ELEONORA GENDLER,
Tel Aviv, Israel / Brooklyn, NY

Bows, buds, flowers, and bugs create a unique collage of earthy appliqués on solid ground. Apparently cut out from lace and printed fabrics, the motifs are applied with bilateral symmetry in general, then gently softened with uneven application of detail mixed in.

TATIANA PARFIONOVA COLLECTION,
Moscow, Russia

Over a neutral, semisheer, matte base, reflective opacity takes a single, winglike motif into various dynamic forms and scales in bilateral symmetry.

SITA MURT,
Madrid, Spain

col·lec·tion \ kə-'lek-shən \ *n*
2: A group of objects or works to be seen, studied, or kept together. **3:** (Clothing & Fashion) a selection of clothes, esp as presented by a particular designer for a specific season.

26

A design collection usually addresses a season, a lifestyle, a specific group of fabrics for a specific price point around an idea or theme, for a target customer. The theme may be visual, conceptual, or color based. A collection will often reflect the time

in which it was created, whether through technological, color, or silhouette trends or visual content, although a collection will have a universal quality if it is made to last beyond trends.

Most designers design and produce collections. Although one-of-a-kind and unique pieces can hold a higher value for their labor and uniqueness, pieces that are presented and created together reflect a particular complex design process involving functionality and cohesion that is engaging for the viewer, the buyer, and the designer or design team. Collections offer options within a temporal theme and are usually produced in quantity with a set of fabrics and shapes selected for that season. A broad line or collection enables the designer to reach a wider audience with more options.

A theme, a shape, an art movement, a new fabric manipulation, embroidery, color, motif, treatment, or construction technique may play across garments in a collection to make it cohesive. A group of textures, prints, a historical or cultural reference, exploration of a silhouette, or attempts to solve a specific design problem could also form the basis for a collection. Choosing a selection (continued on page 212)

Four-piece outerwear collection, gouache. Pictured are four unique silhouettes in two fabrics, with contrast yellow lining. Front and back views emphasize horizontal bands, while minimal seams and edges in arcs or S-curves wrap the body in careful silhouettes. The necklines are warm and flattering.

ANNE BORELLI,
Rio de Janeiro, Brazil

Anna Sui's collection includes carefully selected stripes and patterns in a variety of weights, designed to be layered together in endless variations of print, pattern, direction, and silhouette for her customer.

Anna Sui

NEW YORK

Fur, embellishment, embroideries, layered rich prints and textures, knits and wovens, graphic and lively color, themed stories, lace, techniques, trims, folk- and ethnic-feeling placement prints, coordinated print stories, busy construction techniques, multicultural beauty, and fine details: These all describe elements of Anna Sui's collection. She knows what the fashion public seems to be craving: gorgeous, quality clothes with fantasy built in. Freedom of expression, eclectic mixing, and the antidote to mass production of bland, lifeless shapes that change trends from season to season, Sui is well versed in fashion's languages and offers up a visual, textural, technical, and cultural richness to her audience.

Sui was born in Detroit, Michigan. Her father was an engineer and her mother studied painting. She says she got business smarts from her father and artistic talents from her mother. From both of her parents, she credits her global point of view: Her parents traveled Europe for three years together before she was born and also taught her about Chinese culture. Her mother sewed, and she would take the young Sui fabric shopping with her. Sui learned how patterns work by watching her mother and trying out ideas on her dolls until she was ready to make her own clothes. She admits to having had the fairy-tale vision of the designer's life: swatches, sketchbook, life in Paris, and glamour. She read an article about two young women who went to Parsons School of Design and became successful designers and decided to follow suit.

In her second year, she overheard some students discussing a job opportunity at Charlie's Girls with Erica Elias. She ran over with her portfolio and landed the job. It was a perfect first job: She was giv-

en her own design room with a draper and seamstresses. The company did swimwear, sportswear, and sweaters, so that experience, along with Elias's name, opened many opportunities for her with the big sportswear houses in New York.

In 1981, she started her business out of a corner of her apartment (that eventually took over), then rented an office in the garment district. She had to take extra design jobs to support her company, and every dollar she made went right back into the business.

Ten years later, she staged her first show. It brought in lots of international press and interest from Japanese stores wanting to carry American designers. She decided to go with Isetan, who made her name famous in Asia and opened freestanding Anna Sui boutiques in Japan.

As a designer, she works the show with styling and accessories but makes sure that under it all are really great and lasting pieces. Her work is nostalgic, textural, feminine, vibrant, detailed, and very hip.

A collection brings together a unique color and fabric story. This one layers printed fabrics, sheers, asymmetrical lace, light suitings, and floral-hued solids for an emotive group of separates and dresses.

DEVOTA Y LOMBA, BY MODESTO & LUIS DEVOTA, *Madrid, Spain*

Warm, creamy pastels come together with cool accent colors and metallic gold for a street-to-evening separates collection. From body-baring to boxy, cheetah and tiger motifs and print and embellished belting join the pieces visually along with lamé fabrics, jewelry and gilded aspects, and jewelrylike references in the garments themselves. Fluid and crisp fabrics all come together for this group in a range of proportions, ideas, and techniques.

MANISH ARORA, *New Delhi, India*

of fabrics and trims from which to build the collection is probably the most defining factor. Presenting clothing collections, depending on how they are worked out, can encourage or discourage the customer to pick up more than one piece. A collection of interchangeable and varied pieces will encourage consumers to gather and creatively mix the pieces with each other and their existing wardrobe, while a group of dresses or repeating colors and lengths might be too redundant to warrant purchasing more than one piece.

Seasonal collections can be approached many ways. Some designers wisely build each

Nkhensani Nkosi, designer of South African brand Stoned Cherrie, in her studio surrounded by coordinating samples from her collection of dresses and separates. Behind her, minibodies, fabric and color swatches, print development, and inspiration are all laid out together to plan a unified group of merchandise for the season.

NKHENSANI NKOSI,
Johannesburg, South Africa

This collection offers
structured versus flowing
pieces, square versus flared
hemlines, and a variety of
lengths and options for
different lifestyle situations.
The consumer can mix pieces,
color-blocking silhouettes
and creating outfits to meet
their lifestyle needs. This
variety offers freedom of
expression and utility to
the wearer.

REBECCA MINKOFF,
New York, NY, USA

This backstage layout board presents a tight, cohesive, unisex, urban coastal summer collection around a sunsetlike gradient stripe theme. A photographic sunset print joins pure, simple separates in crisp wovens and stretchy knit fabrics.

OSKLEN, BY USKAR METSAVAHT,
Rio de Janeiro, Brazil

FIRSTVIEW.COM

collection in a way that can be worked with pieces from former collections for a lasting style of classics (whether the style be "classic" or not), while other designers change gears with color, design, or trendiness so drastically from one season to the next that clothes from previous collections may become obsolete.

For big-name designers, collection refers to their definitive top-tier designer line, most in line with their unique vision. It is also their highest priced and most detailed, using the best fabric qualities, finishes, and techniques. Of course, most of these designers have several lower-priced lines so that they can reach a wider client base.

Gouache illustration series. Seven looks comprise a collection of layered and structured pieces to create designer-crafted silhouettes in a range of coordinated fabrics that hold it all together.

CAROLINE ROSSIGNOL,
France/New York, NY, USA

apex:
the point of maximum fullness or measurement of a body form such as the bust

A-line:
a silhouette that anchors to the body in a fitted form, expanding to a fuller, wider hem

batik:
a technique that uses wax to resist garment dye to create surface patterns

bodice:
a garment or garment area that fits through the waist up to the bust or shoulders

boning:
a piece of metal or plastic that supports a garment vertically to keep it smooth and resist collapsing

border:
an edge of a ribbon, fabric, pattern, or decoration that follows a textile hem or cut edge

brocade:
a woven fabric with a raised pattern that is woven into it, often with metallic or colored threads

center front/back:
an actual or imaginary line running vertically down the center of a body or garment

clean finish:
an edge or seam that is faced or finished smoothly or imperceptibly

contour:
an edge perceived as a line in drawing, or any edge of a garment piece or outline

cowl:
a loose drape of excess fabric that runs horizontally and falls vertically, with the maximum weight and fullness between two anchor points, usually centered on the garment bias

crochet:
a technique of creating fabric or lace with a hook that builds chains of loops, one at a time

dart:
seen as a line on a garment from an edge into the garment piece, it is a triangle on a pattern piece that, when stitched, navigates from fullness to fit along a garment silhouette

double-faced fabric:
a fabric that is finished to have two "right sides"

draping:
the tradition and technique of folding, pinning, and controlling fabric panels over the human body form or dress form.

dress form:
(or mannequin) a human-sized body created for draping and fitting fashion garments and patterns, and able to be pinned into securely

Dutch wax/English wax/ imi-wax:
Dutch, English, and African fabric traditions created for the African fashion market using batik and resist techniques and effects to create a crackled base in a unique style

excess:
fabric fullness that is not pulled smoothly against the body like a skin

exposed seams:
seams that are ostentatiously visible from the outside of the garment

facing:
a construction technique or pattern piece in which two matching edges are sewn right sides together, and then turned to create a clean finished edge with the facing inside the garment

flare:
a curved edge that fits a seam smoothly but at its hem ripples with triangular excess forms

gather:
an excess length of fabric that is squeezed into a fitted edge, seam, drawstring, or elastic

gauge:
the size or weight of a yarn or fabric within the available range

gore:
a vertically oriented panel in a series of panels building a garment around the body

gouache:
a type of watercolor pigment containing gum arabic available in tubes or pans, rendering a rich, opaque, velvety texture. A high-level of tempera paints

handkerchief hem:
square corners that follow the grain or edges of a fabric panel

ikat:
a technique of surface pattern treatment that involves binding or waxing some of the warp or weft threads (or even both, in Japanese double ikat) for resist dying before finishing the weaving process

jersey:
a fine gauge machine knitted fabric that is flexible and drapey, generally designed to be cut and sewn into finish garments although seamless garments are also made of a jersey construction

knit:
a flexible fabric form created by rows of interlocking yarn loops rendering stretch flexibility horizontally but not vertically. Fine or chunky yarns or needles can be used in different combinations for different effects, as well as variations of color, cable, and lace stitch forms. Executed by machine or by hand on four (for circular knit) or two needles

look:
a total fashion concept from head to toe including garments, grooming, and accessories

manipulation:
in patternmaking, draping, or construction, refers to the control and improvisation upon pattern shapes and fabric excesses on and around the human form or garment piece

matte:
having a porous, nonreflective surface

natural fiber:
natural components used to make felts or yarns for textiles, such as cotton, linen, hemp, wool, etc

pannier:
from the French word for basket, a pannier is a constructed web of bones that create a large dome shaped skirt and support the fabric

pleat:
a fold in fabric

princess line/princess seam:
a vertical seam that starts at the shoulder, neck, or armhole seam and passes through or near the bust apex and through to the waist or hip to create a fitted or semi-fitted silhouette from panels

production:
the process, facility, and methods used to construct, embellish, and complete fashion garments

proportion:
the relationship between different parts within a whole. Proportion is a truthful observation, but creating pleasing aesthetic relationships in a composition or design is based on the designer's or wearer's opinion and choice

raglan seam/raglan line:
an armhole seam that runs from the underarm into the neckline in order to attach a sleeve to a bodice, instead of encircling the shoulder as in a traditional sleeve.

ribbing:
a knitted pattern of alternating knit and purl stitches that produces a flexible and pronounced vertical pattern that lies flat and does not roll at the hem, commonly used for the neckline, waistband, and cuffs on garments

ruffle:
a gathered or flared panel that creates a row or rows of fullness and texture applied to the surface or hems of garments

set-in-sleeve:
a traditional tailored sleeve construction that fits a sleeve into an armhole, usually with ease in the sleeve cap as in a jacket

S-curve:
a principle of design in which a sweeping curve movement resolves itself by sweeping back in the opposite direction, creating an S-shaped curve that is balanced and lively

scale:
consistent relative proportion of a design no matter what size its representation takes

screen print:
a technique in which cutouts from silk screen panels, as in stenciling, are used to apply designed motifs to the surface of a fabric as a localized decoration, not as an allover repeated pattern

seam finish:
the method, by hand or machine, that is used to protect the cut edges of garment panels that have been joined together, such as overcasting, binding, or overlocking

seam:
the line where two or more panels of fabric have been joined, typically by a row of stitching

shift:
a basic fitted dress that follows the body's shape through seams and other construction details

side seam:
a seam often found running down the sides of a garment, whether straight or curved, fitted or loose, separating front from back and a common location for closures or slits/vents

slash and spread:
a patternmaking technique that takes a basic pattern sloper such as a sleeve or skirt pattern and cuts across it, expanding the slashed shape at one or both ends, to add fabric volume to the pattern piece and create a variation

sloper:
a basic fitted pattern piece that has been tested, fitted, and corrected in order to form the basis for new, functioning pattern design variations

stretch fabrics:
woven or knit fabrics containing elastic fibers such as rubber, Spandex, or Lycra

suiting:
a fabric weight or texture intended for use in suit construction

sustainability:
a design philosophy and necessity that includes renewable resources, recycling and recycled raw materials, conscious consideration of the production, life, care and disposal of a garment and its impact on natural resources and the people it employs

synthetic filament/fiber/ fabric:
long or short fabric components extruded from plastics/polymers and felted, woven, knitted, or formed into fabrics or textiles such as polyester or vinyl

technical drawing/flat sketch:
a line drawing that explicitly shows the overall shape and design construction details of a garment, such as seams, closures, pockets, and other details

topstitching:
row or rows of stitching visible from the outside of a garment, decorative and/or functional

tier:
a horizontal layer or panel of fabric that may be attached to the row above it or to an understructure

tunic:
a shirt or dress garment shape that embodies the torso, ending around the hip level

twill:
a woven fabric such as denim that produces a diagonally textured surface

About the Author

Laura Volpintesta was born in Mexico City and raised in Bethel, Connecticut, completing her BFA at Parsons School of Design, NYC, in 1995 with one amazing year in Paris surrounded by French couture, Japanese avant-garde, and African prints and tailoring. Born to gringo parents (in Mexico City) and Italian immigrant grandparents, she has always been curious about cultural cross-pollination as well as the immigrant experience while growing up. Her parents' love of classical, contemporary, and folkloric world music, literature, languages, and painting culminated in her landing at Parsons New York City in 1991.

In 1997, leaving New York after a season at Old Navy and setting up her private studio alongside CT's Brazilian community, which influenced her greatly, she was invited by Marie Essex to teach patternmaking, draping, and construction methods in Parsons' BFA program. Teaching illustration and concept-development classes part time turned into a full-time faculty position while freelancing as a sketch artist and technical designer/samplemaker in NYC's garment center at various design houses.

She has enthusiastically taught fashion illustration, portfolio development, model drawing, and concept development to over a thousand international students from beginner to graduating level. In 2008, she created Parsons' first entirely online fashion design studio course, which still runs today.

She now resides in Connecticut where she homeschools her three children and is the founder of FashionIllustrationTribe.com, a growing online fashion design education and research community.

Also a doula and singer, she records and performs with jazz and Brazilian artists, advocates for women's rights in maternal healthcare, and spends the majority of her time writing, researching, and teaching from home.

ACKNOWLEDGMENTS

I never could have imagined the depth, breadth, and scope of the journey that this project has taken me on. When I started working on it, I created one little folder on my desktop called "dream" because I didn't want to forget, as the subfolders multiplied a hundredfold, that all of this work was truly born of a crazy, massive dream that brought me to Parsons to study fashion design in the first place. Embarking on this research created a single line of continuity from the deep love of an aspiring young woman of twenty with that of a mother of three, accomplished teacher and artist/artisan at forty, connecting the dots in between.

Thank you *American Elle* magazine, 1985–1995, (including Azzedine Alaia, Issey Miyake, Jean Paul Gaultier, Martin Margiela, Gilles Bensimon, Irving Penn, and all others inside.) You taught me the Language of Fashion. Thank you, Grandma Angelina Serpe Volpintesta, for my first subscription and never-ending love and support. Your love is woven into the pages of this book.

Thank you, Mom and Howard, for always believing in me and supporting me physically and emotionally, day to day, as needed, and for helping me to birth every one of my babies, including this one. Mom and Aunts Mary, Susan, and Maureen, who are each unique fashion icons, mothers, and artists like my grandma, Ines Tango Casey, each one of them.

Thank you, Dad and Nami, for your constant support of my dreams, and for sending me to Paris in spite of everything. Thank you Rob, Erin, Emily, Farrah, Rosie, Rocco. Bonnie, for your huge heart and visionary community. David, Leila, Andy and Michelle, You are my family and my inspiration.

My biggest inspirations: My children, Lua and Lorenzo ... as if having little Angelina Volpintesta II come along wasn't enough, and then comes this book! No one can quite imagine how patient you were, how intense the deadlines were, how many meals and dishes and toddler messes had to pile up while I burned the day and midnight oil. Still, I'm so thankful that I was able to write it in your precious presence. Clara Domingas, Dinna Soliman, Eva Leticia Padilla, Silvia Merlin Lucente, Maria Jose Palmeira, Taty Tokas, Michele Nascimento-Kettner, Christianne Leite, Kathy Maggio, Doo Ri Chung, Fernanda Yamamoto, Maria Bassaro-Delcampe, Emma "Mimi" Tetteh, and Joni Stone, women each with their own arts, songs, and stories tied into mine in a special, inextricable way. Alexandrino DuCarmo, Ronaldo Fraga (whom I've never met yet), and Dona Nene Maria da Paixao Texeira in Belo Horizonte, Minas Gerais, Brazil, for helping me to experience high art in such pure forms.

Thank you Emily Potts, my editor, for inviting me repeatedly and guiding me gently on this project that became a total revival and redirection to my research and career in the world of fashion. Betsy Gammons, and Cora Hawks at Rockport Publishers, thank you for your utmost patience, support, organization, and good cheer!

The late Marie Essex for giving me the amazing freedom and satisfaction that comes from sharing my gifts through teaching. You knew how much I would love to teach—thank you for recognizing this in me! I had always dreamed of working in a "fashion laboratory." You made this a reality. Pamela Trought-Klein, for your mentoring. Sistamama Kristie Liotta, for your constant support, tea, passion, and affirmation.

Pastor Jackson et al, for the year's journey of prayer, hope, and encouragement. Gabby Bernstein for miracles (like this project), Marie Forleo for supporting women like me in business. Bethel Homeschooling Meetup Group for reminding me I'm a mom first and keeping me surrounded and inspired.

For every designer who contributed, and I lament that I couldn't include every piece that I wanted. Thank you to every inspired and beautiful student, past and future, who shared their dream with me over fifteen weeks, I carry each one of you deep in my heart for sharing your first steps, fears, beauty, and dreams, with me. To designers with courageous hearts that bring about change through a vision with love. Thank you to Brazilian, African, Jazz, and Gospel artists who have fed my soul with your gifts. Thank you, dear God, for my gifts and the opportunities to use them and mothers and aunties everywhere, who quietly make their ways to keep their families afloat, straddling family and work to care for their children, thank you. That fashion may remember to serve you in every way, more each day, including Mother Earth.

COLOPHON

The Language of Fashion Design was designed and typeset by Poulin + Morris Inc., New York, New York. Digital type composition, page layouts, and type design were originated on Apple iMac computers, utilizing Adobe InDesign CS5.5, Version 7.5.3 software.

The text of the book was set in Verlag and Archer, two typefaces designed and produced by Hoefler & Frere-Jones, New York, New York.